Getting Started with React Native

Learn to build modern native iOS and Android applications using JavaScript and the incredible power of React

Ethan Holmes

Tom Bray

BIRMINGHAM - MUMBAI

Getting Started with React Native

First published: December 2015

Production reference: 1101215

Published by Packt Publishing Ltd.
Livery Place
35 Livery Street
Birmingham B3 2PB, UK.

ISBN 978-1-78588-518-1

www.packtpub.com

Credits

Authors
Ethan Holmes

Tom Bray

Reviewer
Soliury

Content Manager
Wilson Dsouza

Acquisition Editor
Aaron Lazar

Content Development Editor
Divij Kotian

Technical Editor
Naveenkumar Jain

Copy Editor
Sneha Singh

Project Coordinator
Nikhil Nair

Proofreader
Safis Editing

Indexer
Hemangini Bari

Graphics
Kirk D'Penha

Production Coordinator
Shantanu N. Zagade

Cover Work
Shantanu N. Zagade

About the Authors

Ethan Holmes is a Software Engineer from Vancouver, BC, Canada. He obtained a B.Sc. in computer science from Simon Fraser University. He has primarily been a full-stack web developer working and creating applications for start-ups in the Silicon Beach area. Currently, he is stationed at Cargomatic, disrupting the freight industry. After learning React for the web, learning React Native complemented the skills he obtained as a web developer and allowed him to quickly make the transition to mobile development.

You can follow him on Twitter at `@sherclockholmes`.

I'd like to thank Tom for being such a great ol' chap and for giving me the opportunity to work on this book with him. Big thanks to the friends and colleagues I have met throughout my many years of software development. Shout out to my Bengal cat, Whiskey!

Tom Bray has been developing for the web since the browser wars of the late 90s when DHTML was the buzzword of the day. Creating great user experiences using the cutting edge technologies of the day has always been his passion, from Flash to Flex to Adobe AIR to React, and React Native.

He has created sophisticated software that has been used by large companies, such as Adobe, MySpace, Cisco, Informatica, and Dell; it has been a key contributor to numerous start-ups where he has worn many hats and gained a broad skill set. He currently serves as the Principal Software Architect with Cargomatic where he has designed a system to orchestrate the movement of ocean freight to and from America's ports—a solution that leveraged React Native to assign work to truck drivers and track their progress.

You can follow him on Twitter at `@tombray`.

I would like to dedicate this book to my wonderful wife, Amy, and my amazing son, Tyler. They have put up with me working late at night and on weekends, and I couldn't have written this book without their love and support. They bring me great joy and I'm so grateful to have them in my life.

I also want to thank my co-author, Ethan Holmes, who is a fantastic developer, a great writer, and an exemplary Canadian. His hard work and dedication were crucial in making this book a reality in a short amount of time. Thank you, Ethan!

About the Reviewer

Soliury is a frontend engineer from China. He is now working in Meituan and he loves JavaScript. He is excited to see that React Native is getting more and more popular. He also writes react-native apps for `http://cnodejs.org`. His GitHub ID is `https://github.com/soliury`.

I would like to thank my girlfriend, Jennifer, who has supported my work and also understands me. I would also like to thank Nikhil for helping me when I am busy.

www.PacktPub.com

Support files, eBooks, discount offers, and more

For support files and downloads related to your book, please visit www.PacktPub.com.

Did you know that Packt offers eBook versions of every book published, with PDF and ePub files available? You can upgrade to the eBook version at www.PacktPub.com and, as a print book customer, you are entitled to a discount on the eBook copy. Get in touch with us at service@packtpub.com for more details.

At www.PacktPub.com, you can also read a collection of free technical articles, sign up for a range of free newsletters and receive exclusive discounts and offers on Packt books and eBooks.

https://www2.packtpub.com/books/subscription/packtlib

Do you need instant solutions to your IT questions? PacktLib is Packt's online digital book library. Here, you can search, access, and read Packt's entire library of books.

Why subscribe?

- Fully searchable across every book published by Packt
- Copy and paste, print, and bookmark content
- On demand and accessible via a web browser

Free access for Packt account holders

If you have an account with Packt at www.PacktPub.com, you can use this to access PacktLib today and view 9 entirely free books. Simply use your login credentials for immediate access.

Table of Contents

Preface

Why are there so many alternatives to using native languages to write mobile apps? And, more importantly, why does the world need yet another approach? Obviously, there must be a problem that hasn't been solved.

Developers want to use just one language to develop for both iOS and Android. Web developers want to reuse their existing JavaScript knowledge and leverage the web frameworks they already know and love. This is why Apache Cordova (PhoneGap) exists. By wrapping a web browser in a native app, developers can package their HTML, CSS, and JavaScript applications in a native shell, but why aren't all mobile applications based on Cordova?

Users expect native performance, with a native user experience. Hybrid apps don't solve the user's problems, they solve the developer's problems. We need a technology that can do both!

React Native changes the game with applications that are truly native. It doesn't use a WebView or transpile JavaScript to native languages. Think of it as native UI components being controlled by a JavaScript brain. The result is a user experience that is indistinguishable from any other native app, and a developer experience that leverages the amazing productivity benefits of JavaScript and the React framework.

Armed with React Native, you'll finally be able to leverage your web development skills in the mobile world without sacrificing quality or performance. It's the Holy Grail, and we're excited to show you what React Native can do and to see what amazing apps you create with it!

What this book covers

Chapter 1, Exploring the Sample Application, is a step-by-step guide to running the sample iOS Application.

Chapter 2, Understanding React Native Fundamentals, covers the basics of React Native and gives brief insight into how the Virtual DOM improves performance. Then there is an introduction to props and state by creating your first component.

Chapter 3, Beginning with the Example Application, begins with generating the project files for iOS and Android. Then it continues with creating the first screens and adding navigation to the application.

Chapter 4, Working with Styles and Layout, covers the ins and outs of laying out and styling content in React Native. Learn how to apply React CSS and Flexbox to your components.

Chapter 5, Displaying and Saving Data, uses ListViews to display data and save notes using the AsyncStorage API.

Chapter 6, Working with Geolocation and Maps, discusses the geolocation API and Map Component.

Chapter 7, Integrating Native Modules, focuses on integrating third party native modules from the React Native community into your applications.

Chapter 8, Releasing the Application, goes through the release process for iOS and Android so you are ready to submit an application to the AppStore or the Google Play Store.

What you need for this book

The software requirements for this book are as follows:

- Xcode
- Command Line Tools
- npm 2.x
- JDK
- Android SDK

Who this book is for

This book is for web developers who want to learn to build fast, good-looking, native mobile applications using the skills they already have. If you already have some JavaScript knowledge or are using React on the web, then you will be able to quickly get up and running with React Native for iOS and Android.

Conventions

In this book, you will find a number of text styles that distinguish between different kinds of information. Here are some examples of these styles and an explanation of their meaning.

Code words in text, database table names, folder names, filenames, file extensions, pathnames, dummy URLs, user input, and Twitter handles are shown as follows: "Open the ReactNotes.xcodeproj in the ios/ folder in Xcode."

A block of code is set as follows:

```
NSURL *jsCodeLocation;

/**
 * Loading JavaScript code - uncomment the one you want.
 *
 * OPTION 1
 * Load from development server. Start the server from the repository
 root:
 *
 * $ npm start
 *
 * To run on device, change `localhost` to the IP address of your
 computer
 * (you can get this by typing `ifconfig` into the terminal and
 selecting the
 * `inet` value under `en0:`) and make sure your computer and iOS
 device are
 * on the same Wi-Fi network.
 */
```

When we wish to draw your attention to a particular part of a code block, the relevant lines or items are set in bold:

```
/**
* OPTION 2
* Load from pre-bundled file on disk. To re-generate the static bundle
* from the root of your project directory, run
*
* $ react-native bundle --minify
*
* see http://facebook.github.io/react-native/docs/runningondevice.html
*/

//jsCodeLocation = [[NSBundle mainBundle] URLForResource:@"main"
withExtension:@"jsbundle"];
```

Any command-line input or output is written as follows:

```
# cp /usr/src/asterisk-addons/configs/cdr_mysql.conf.sample
    /etc/asterisk/cdr_mysql.conf
```

New terms and **important words** are shown in bold. Words that you see on the screen, for example, in menus or dialog boxes, appear in the text like this: "Select **Run** and under the **Info** tab change **Build Configuration** from **Release** to **Debug**."

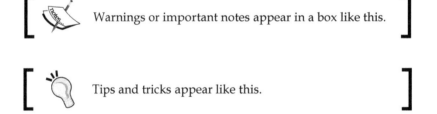

Warnings or important notes appear in a box like this.

Tips and tricks appear like this.

Reader feedback

Feedback from our readers is always welcome. Let us know what you think about this book—what you liked or disliked. Reader feedback is important for us as it helps us develop titles that you will really get the most out of.

To send us general feedback, simply e-mail feedback@packtpub.com, and mention the book's title in the subject of your message.

If there is a topic that you have expertise in and you are interested in either writing or contributing to a book, see our author guide at www.packtpub.com/authors.

Customer support

Now that you are the proud owner of a Packt book, we have a number of things to help you to get the most from your purchase.

Downloading the example code

You can download the example code files from your account at http://www.packtpub.com for all the Packt Publishing books you have purchased. If you purchased this book elsewhere, you can visit http://www.packtpub.com/support and register to have the files e-mailed directly to you.

Downloading the color images of this book

We also provide you with a PDF file that has color images of the screenshots/diagrams used in this book. The color images will help you better understand the changes in the output. You can download this file from http://www.packtpub.com/sites/default/files/downloads/Getting Started with React Native_ColorImages.pdf.

Errata

Although we have taken every care to ensure the accuracy of our content, mistakes do happen. If you find a mistake in one of our books—maybe a mistake in the text or the code—we would be grateful if you could report this to us. By doing so, you can save other readers from frustration and help us improve subsequent versions of this book. If you find any errata, please report them by visiting http://www.packtpub.com/submit-errata, selecting your book, clicking on the **Errata Submission Form** link, and entering the details of your errata. Once your errata are verified, your submission will be accepted and the errata will be uploaded to our website or added to any list of existing errata under the Errata section of that title.

To view the previously submitted errata, go to https://www.packtpub.com/books/content/support and enter the name of the book in the search field. The required information will appear under the **Errata** section.

Piracy

Piracy of copyrighted material on the Internet is an ongoing problem across all media. At Packt, we take the protection of our copyright and licenses very seriously. If you come across any illegal copies of our works in any form on the Internet, please provide us with the location address or website name immediately so that we can pursue a remedy.

Please contact us at copyright@packtpub.com with a link to the suspected pirated material.

We appreciate your help in protecting our authors and our ability to bring you valuable content.

Questions

If you have a problem with any aspect of this book, you can contact us at questions@packtpub.com, and we will do our best to address the problem.

1

Exploring the Sample Application

React Native is beginning to change the game in the mobile development world. Using the skills you already have, as a web developer, you can get a set of familiar methods to build user interfaces for mobile devices. In this book, we'll walk you through many React Natives features while developing a *note-taking* application, which we call **React Notes**. While building the essential features, such as creating notes, saving notes to the device, viewing a list of saved notes, and navigating between screens, you'll learn the fundamental skills you need to develop an app of your own. You'll also have the opportunity to go beyond the basics by adding the ability to store images and geolocation data with notes. Functionality is only a part of what makes a great app — it has to be great looking as well, so we've made sure to equip you with a thorough understanding of layout and styles. By the end of the book, you will have developed a fully featured application from start to finish and have all the skills you need to share your React Native applications with the world!

In this chapter, we'll introduce you to React Notes, the sample application that you'll learn how to build. We'll even point you in the right direction if you're anxious to start tinkering with the sample app to see what happens.

This chapter will focus on the following:

- Installing Xcode on Mac OS X
- Running the sample application in the iOS simulator
- Taking a look at the sample application features
- Modifying the sample application

Installing Xcode

Getting the tools to run the sample application is simple in OS X. The easiest way to install Xcode is through the App Store. In the top right-hand bar, search for the term **Xcode**, and from the list of results navigate to the Xcode store page, as shown in the following screenshot:

Install or update to the latest version of Xcode by clicking on the button.

 You will need to register for an Apple ID in order to download Xcode from the App Store.

You also require the **command-line tools** (CLT) for Xcode. A prompt will display when they need to be installed. You can also download the command-line tools directly from the **Downloads** for Apple developers at `https://developer.apple.com/downloads/`.

Running the sample application

The source code contains the completed application that we will build throughout the book. We are going to start with running the application. The source code is already configured to run in the iOS simulator:

1. Open the `ReactNotes.xcodeproj` in the `ios/` folder in Xcode or from the command line:

```
ReactNotes$ open ios/ReactNotes.xcodeproj/
```

Downloading the example code

You can download the example code files from your account at `http://www.packtpub.com` for all the Packt Publishing books you have purchased. If you purchased this book elsewhere, you can visit `http://www.packtpub.com/support` and register to have the files e-mailed directly to you.

2. This book targets iPhone 6 for development; although it does work on other iOS versions, we recommend using this one. Make sure that the iPhone 6 is selected in the iOS simulator device drop-down menu. If you own an iPhone 6, you may select an **iOS Device**:

3. Press the **Run** button (*F5*) to launch the iOS simulator:

A sneak peek at the sample application

The goal of this book is to introduce you to how quickly React Native can get you up and running to create user interfaces. No matter what type of mobile application you build, there are certain features that you're very likely to have. Your UI will probably have multiple screens, so you'll need the ability to navigate between them. In *Chapter 3, Beginning with the Example Application* we will start laying the foundation for navigation and the note screen:

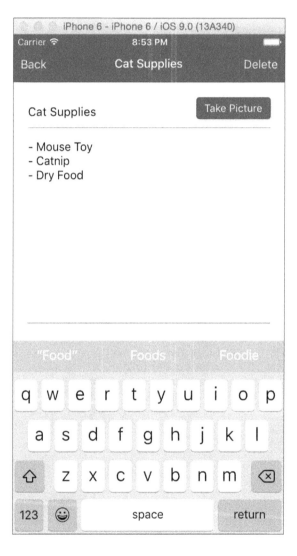

Not long after you have seen a bare-bones application, you'll want to start making it look good. Let us dive deep into styles and layout in *Chapter 4, Working with Styles and Layout*, and carry those lessons throughout the rest of the book.

It's hard to imagine an application that doesn't have lists of data, and React Notes is no exception. We'll cover working with lists in *Chapter 5, Displaying and Saving Data*:

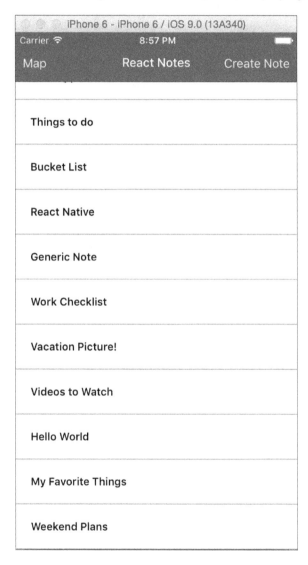

One of the capabilities that sets mobile applications apart from web applications is the ability to access GPS data. We present capturing geolocation data using maps in *Chapter 6, Working with Geolocation and Maps*:

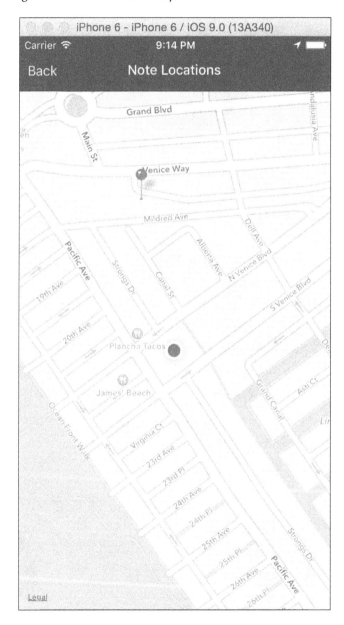

It is very common to capture photos on mobile devices. The camera screen will allow users to attach photos to their notes and save them for viewing later. You will learn how to add camera support to your applications in *Chapter 7, Using Native Modules*:

 Note that the camera screen will be black in the iOS simulator. This is also explained later in *Chapter 7, Using Native Modules*.

Experimenting with the sample application

If you are the adventurous type, then feel free to start playing around and modifying the sample application code. There are two steps to switch the iOS application into development mode:

1. Open the `AppDelegate.m` file in Xcode and uncomment the `jsCodeLocation` assignment from OPTION 1 and comment out the statement in OPTION 2:

```
NSURL *jsCodeLocation;

/**
 * Loading JavaScript code - uncomment the one you want.
 *
 * OPTION 1
 * Load from development server. Start the server from the
 repository root:
 *
 * $ npm start
 *
 * To run on device, change `localhost` to the IP address of your
 computer
 * (you can get this by typing `ifconfig` into the terminal and
 selecting the
 * `inet` value under `en0:`) and make sure your computer and iOS
 device are
 * on the same Wi-Fi network.
 */

jsCodeLocation = [NSURL URLWithString:@"http://localhost:8081/
index.ios.bundle?platform=ios"];

/**
 * OPTION 2
 * Load from pre-bundled file on disk. To re-generate the static
 bundle
 * from the root of your project directory, run
 *
 * $ react-native bundle --minify
 *
```

```
* see http://facebook.github.io/react-native/docs/runningondevice.
html
*/

//jsCodeLocation = [[NSBundle mainBundle] URLForResource:@"main"
withExtension:@"jsbundle"];
```

2. Then, navigate to **Product | Scheme | Edit Scheme...**. Select **Run**, and under the **Info** tab change **Build Configuration** from **Release** to **Debug**, as shown:

3. **Run** (*F5*) from Xcode to start the application in development mode. Using the `Shake` gesture from the iOS simulator (**Hardware | Shake | Gesture**) will show the development menu. It may be necessary to run `react-native start` from the command line to load the JavaScript bundle.

That's it! From here you can freely modify any of the source code in `index.ios.js` or in the `Components` folder. Later we will explain how to quickly reload your code in the simulator without having to recompile from Xcode.

Summary

This chapter gave us a brief overview of the type of functionality and user interface we will introduce throughout the rest of the book. We will cover features such as navigation, lists, user inputs, and so on in depth. With Xcode already set up, you will be able to jump right in to iOS development, and for Android developers we begin the setup in *Chapter 3, Beginning with the Example Application*. Next, we will demonstrate the value that React Native offers in rapid mobile development using the skills you have learned as a web developer.

Let's get started!

2
Understanding React Native Fundamentals

You might not be familiar with how React for Web works, so we are going to cover the fundamentals in this chapter. We will also explain the core principles of how React for Web works under the hood. Once you have a solid understanding of the basics, we will dive into how React for Web works and the subtle differences between mobile and web. By the end of this chapter, you will have the necessary skills to start building the example application.

In this chapter we will cover the following topics:

- The Virtual DOM
- Introducing components and JSX
- Writing our first component
- Props and state of components

The Virtual DOM

Do you know how to write a JavaScript function? If you do, that's great! You're well on your way to understand how React and React Native work under the hood. What do we mean exactly? Well, when you research how React works, you'll eventually encounter someone explaining it in the following manner:

```
UI = f(data)
```

You may say, *Nerd alert! How is this helpful?* Well, it's saying that your UI is a function of your data. To put it in more familiar terms, let's say that:

```
var todos = function(data) { return data.join( " -- " ) }
```

You can call the `function` with an array of data, such as:

```
var ui = todos( ["wake up", "get out of bed", "drag a comb across my
head"] );
console.log(ui);
```

This is not a particularly earth-shattering code; however, you're now rendering some content, in this case to the console.

What if, all your UI rendering code could be this predictable? It can be! Let's start getting a little more advanced. What if, in addition to our `todos()` function, we had a function called `todoItem()`, such as:

```
var todoItem = function(data) { return "<strong>" + data + "</strong>"
}
```

That looks a lot like our original `UI` function, doesn't it?:

```
UI = f(data)
```

What if we start composing our `todos()` and `todoItems()`, such as:

```
var ui = todos( [todoItem("wake up"), todoItem("get out of bed")] );
```

You can start to get the picture that we can start to render more and more complex outputs by composing simple functions.

What if we want to start rendering our content to the browser? I'm sure you can imagine changing our `todoItem()` to add elements to the DOM using jQuery; however, in this case we will start repeating ourselves a lot with many instances of `appendChild()` calls and jQuery selectors. If we are really smart, we might write a framework to abstract away the DOM manipulations so that we can write the code that matters to our application, not just the code that matters to the browser.

OK, so now let's say that we've magically got a framework that lets us represent our UI as a `data` function and we don't have to think about how our content will get rendered to the DOM. We can start changing our data over and over and watch the DOM update! That sounds great in theory, but when we have dozens of `div` elements in a deeply nested hierarchy, the underlying DOM manipulations become complex and inefficient.

What if our magic framework had an intermediate representation of the DOM? Let's call it Virtual DOM and let's say that instead of making every little change to the DOM, we batch the changes together. We can even compare the before and after states of the Virtual DOM. Figure out the differences and reduce the number of real DOM manipulations that we need to perform. Now we're really on to something!

So we can now express our UI as a function of our data. We don't have to think about the underlying DOM manipulation code and our UI is nice and snappy because the underlying framework is really smart and reduces the number of DOM manipulations it needs to perform. It will be pretty great to have a framework that could do that for us, but you know what will be really cool? What if the DOM didn't have to be a browser DOM? What if that same abstraction that allows us to write the code that matters to our app could be used to, say, update native mobile components? Enter React Native.

Components

Now here is an interesting problem; we have come across this great framework for making fast differences between the Virtual DOM and its native components. How do we tell React Native what UI to represent or when to change it? A React Native component is a simple, reusable, function-like object that enables us to describe the native mobile components we want to render. They will always contain properties, state, and a render method. Let's start really simple by creating our own component.

Creating your first component

Creating a new component in React Native will look similar to the following:

```
import React, {
  Text,
  View
  } from 'react-native';
class HelloComponent extends React.Component {
  render () {
    return (
    <View>
      <Text>Hello React</Text>
    <View>
  );
  }
}
```

Remember to import the React Native module. Here, we are using the ES6 import statement; it is similar to how the node require module works.

Wait a second... What are these weird XML elements doing in my JavaScript code? Facebook has created its own syntactic extension over JavaScript to describe React components. Here is the exact same code, but written in ordinary JavaScript:

```
var HelloComponent = React.createClass({displayName:
  "HelloComponent"}, render: function () {
  return (
    React.createElement(View, null,
      React.createElement(Text, null, "Hello React")
  )
));
```

While it is possible to write React Native applications only in JavaScript, the previous syntax includes many added benefits for the developer.

JSX

JavaScript XML (JSX) is an XML-like extension to the ECMAScript specification. It combines the component logic (JavaScript) and markup (DOM or Native UI) into a single file.

A JSX Element will take the following form:

```
var element = (
  <JSXElement>
    <SubJSXElement />
    <SubJSXElement />
    <SubJSXElement />
  <JSXElement />
);
```

The JSX specification also defines the following:

- The JSX Elements can be either self-opening `<JSXElement></JSXElement>` or self-closing `<JSXElement />`.
- Accept attributes as an expression `{}` or string `""` `<Component attr="attribute">`. Expressions are JavaScript snippets.
- The children elements can be text, expressions, or elements.

What if you have more than one component or a list of components?
There can only be a single root element; it means that if you have multiple components, you must wrap them in a parent component.

This is cool! We have gone from a deeply nested and imperative JavaScript code to a declarative format that describes the exact elements that we want to see in our components. There is no separation of concerns since our logic is coupled with our markup, making the components easier to debug and test. Since you can always include the same component in multiple other components, there is no need to duplicate the code anyway.

Note that JSX is only meant to be used as a preprocessor and it is not recommended to transpile in your production build. More information on JSX can be found in the official React documentation `https://facebook.github.io/react/docs/jsx-in-depth.html` or in the official JSX Specification `https://facebook.github.io/jsx/`.

Back to our first component

There are a few things that we have overlooked in our component. **View** and **Text** are two of the many components provided by React Native to build a UI. These are not regular components that render in the JavaScript layer, they can map directly to their native container parts! The View component maps to `UIView` in IOS and `android.view` in Android, while Text is the generic component to display text on each platform respectively. **View** and **Text** support various functions, such as layouts, styling, and touch handling.

Displaying the same static text over and over is not very exciting. Let's extend this simple component and add some more functionalities.

Props and states

At this point, you may be wondering how React Native deals with component manipulation and communication as the number of components grows into a component hierarchy. A component hierarchy, similar to a tree, starts with a root component and can contain many children. React Native provides two methods of data passing; one for data-flow down the component hierarchy and another for maintaining internal state.

Props

How do the components in the same component hierarchy communicate with each other? Data is passed down through properties commonly known as **props**. Props are considered to be immutable by convention and should never be modified directly. To pass a prop into a component, just add a camel-cased attribute to the component:

```
<HelloComponent text="Hello React" />
```

Props can be accessed internally in the component through `this.props`:

```
import React, {
  Text,
  View
} from 'react-native';

class HelloComponent extends React.Component {
  render () {
    return (
      <View>
        <Text>{this.props.text}</Text>
      View>
    );
  }
}
```

What if I want to pass down a lot of props?

It is possible to pass an array of props to a component using the ES7 spread operator `<HelloComponent {...props} />`.

It is not always necessary to include props with a component, but if you require a default value for your props, you can assign the `defaultProps` object to the component's class constructor.

```
HelloComponent.defaultProps = {text: "Default Text!"};
```

Validating props

If you are planning to expose your component to the public, it makes sense to constrain the ways developers can use it. To enforce that your components are being used correctly, the **PropTypes** module can be used to validate any props passed in. In the event that a prop does not pass the `propType` validation, a warning is shown to the developer in the console. The `PropTypes` cover a wide range of JavaScript types and primitives, including nested objects. You can define `propTypes` on a component's class constructor:

```
HelloComponent.propTypes = {text: React.PropTypes.string};
```

For more information on `propTypes`, visit the Prop Validation section of React Docs `https://facebook.github.io/react/docs/reusable-components.html`.

State

So now we can pass in the data, but what if the data changes, then how can we display these changes to the user? Components can optionally contain state, a mutable and private set of data. State is a great way to keep track of user input, asynchronous requests, and events. Let's update our component with additional text when the user interacts with it:

```
import React, {
  Text,
  View,
  Component
  } from 'react-native';
class HelloComponent extends React.Component{
  constructor (props) {
    super(props);
    this.state = {  // Set Initial State
    appendText: ''
  };
}
render () {
  return (
    <View>
      <Text onPress={() => setState({text: ' Native!'})}>{this.
props.text + this.state.appendText}</Text>
      <View>
  );
  }
}
```

Touching the Text component will trigger the function in its onPress prop. We are taking advantage of the ES6 arrow syntax to include our functionality in line with the text component.

 Using the ES6 arrow syntax will automatically bind this to a function. For any non-arrow function, if you need access to this then you need to bind the value to the function in the props expression `<Text onPress={this.myFunction.bind(this)}>`.

The setState function will merge the object you pass into the first argument with the current state of the component. Calling setState will trigger a new render where, instead of being empty, this.state.appendText will append **Native!** to the value of text, which we originally passed in from props. The final result is "Hello React" + " Native!" to produce "Hello React Native!".

Never try and modify the value of this state on your own. Directly changing the state could result in data loss during the next setState call and it will not trigger another re-render.

Summary

Now hopefully, you understand the radical new direction React has taken in achieving performance. The Virtual DOM handles all of the DOM manipulations for us behind the scenes. At the same time, it uses efficient diffing algorithms to minimize the number of calls to the DOM. We have also seen how JSX allows us to express our components declaratively and combine our application logic into a single file. By using props and state, we can pass the data through components and update them dynamically.

I hope you can now take the information you learned in this chapter and convince your boss to start using React Native right away!

Beginning with the Example Application

3

Now that you have an idea about how React Native works and how to create components, let's create your first React Native application. Throughout this book, we will be developing a note-taking application which we'll call **ReactNotes**. By the end of the book, you'll have a fully featured application that allows you to create notes, save them to a device, view the list of the notes you've saved, take pictures with the device and attach them to your notes, and much more.

In this chapter, we'll build the skeleton of the application, create a `HomeScreen` and `NoteScreen`. We'll also add navigation that allows you to switch between the screens, and along the way you'll learn about creating your own components and handling events.

The topics that we will cover in this chapter are:

- How to generate iOS and Android project files
- Examining the React Native starter template
- Creating the first component, `SimpleButton`
- Debugging with Chrome Developer Tools
- Exploring navigation and transitioning between screens
- Developing the UI to create notes

Generating the projects

To start building our note taking application for iOS, we are going to need a couple of command-line tools.

- React Native 0.14.2 requires **Node.js v4+**, we are going to use v5.0.0; visit `https://nodejs.org` for more information (we recommend managing different node versions with NVM `https://github.com/creationix/nvm`)

- Install the latest version of NPM from `https://www.npmjs.com/`

Great, now that we have these tools we can install the `react-native-cli`. The `react-native-cli` exposes an interface that does all the work of setting up a new React Native project for us:

1. To install `react-native-cli`, use the `npm` command:

   ```
   npm install -g react-native-cli
   ```

2. Next, we are going to generate a new React Native project called `ReactNotes` using the `cli` and the `react-native init` command. The output of the command looks similar to the following:

   ```
   $ react-native init ReactNotes
   ```

   This will walk you through the creation of a new React Native project in `/Users/ethanholmes/ReactNotes`.

3. Set up a new React Native app in `/Users/ethanholmes/ReactNotes`:

   ```
   create .flowconfig
   create .gitignore
   create .watchmanconfig
   create index.ios.js
   create index.android.js
   create ios/main.jsbundle
   create ios/ReactNotes/AppDelegate.h
   create ios/ReactNotes/AppDelegate.m
   create ios/ReactNotes/Base.lproj/LaunchScreen.xib
   create ios/ReactNotes/Images.xcassets/AppIcon.
     appiconset/Contents json
   create ios/ReactNotes/Info.plist
   create ios/ReactNotes/main.m
   create ios/ReactNotesTests/ReactNotesTests.m
   create ios/ReactNotesTests/Info.plist
   create ios/ReactNotes.xcodeproj/project.pbxproj
   create ios/ReactNotes.xcodeproj/xcshareddata/xcschemes/
     ReactNotes.xcscheme
   ```

```
create android/app/build.gradle
create android/app/proguard-rules.pro
create android/app/src/main/AndroidManifest.xml
create android/app/src/main/res/values/strings.xml
create android/app/src/main/res/values/styles.xml
create android/build.gradle
create android/gradle.properties
create android/settings.gradle
create android/app/src/main/res/mipmap-
  hdpi/ic_launcher.png
create android/app/src/main/res/mipmap-
  mdpi/ic_launcher.png
create android/app/src/main/res/mipmap-
  xhdpi/ic_launcher.png
create android/app/src/main/res/mipmap-
  xxhdpi/ic_launcher.png
create android/gradle/wrapper/gradle-wrapper.jar
create android/gradle/wrapper/gradle-wrapper.properties
create android/gradlew
create android/gradlew.bat
create android/app/src/main/java/com/reactnotes/
  MainActivity.java
```

To run your app on iOS:

```
Open /Users/ethanholmes/ReactNotes/ios/ReactNotes.xcodeproj in
Xcode
Hit Run button
```

To run your app on Android:

```
Have an Android emulator running, or a device connected
cd /Users/ethanholmes/ReactNotes
react-native run-android
```

The root directory of the Xcode project is generated in the ReactNotes folder, with the same name as we gave react-native-cli when we ran the command. Follow the steps at the end of the React Native set up to see what it produces.

Xcode and the iOS simulator

We are going to start by running the starter template in the iOS simulator through Xcode:

1. In Xcode, select `File | Open` and navigate to the `ReactNotes` folder.

2. Open the `ReactNotes.xcodeproj` file, as shown in the following figure:

3. Click on **Run** (or *Cmd + R*) to run the application in the iOS simulator, the following screenshot will be shown:

Just like that, we already have the React Native template up and running on the iOS simulator!

The Android SDK and emulator

Facebook has a detailed step by step guide set up on Android SDK and emulator. You can access the React Native Docs at `https://facebook.github.io/react-native/docs/android-setup.html`. In this section, we will only cover the basics of running the application on the Android emulator.

When running the project in the iOS simulator, we can run it from the Xcode IDE. Android, on the other hand, doesn't require any particular IDE and can be launched directly from the command line.

To install the `android apk` to the emulator, use the following command:

```
$ react-native run-android
```

The following screenshot will be generated:

Let's start by modifying the contents of the starter template and display a different message.

Modifying the React Native starter template

Open `index.ios.js`, located in the root directory, in the text editor of your choice. Here is the code that `react-native-cli` generated:

```
/**
 * Sample React Native App
 * https://github.com/facebook/react-native
 */
'use strict';

var React = require('react-native');
var {
  AppRegistry,
  StyleSheet,
  Text,
  View,
} = React;

var ReactNotes = React.createClass({
  render: function() {
    return (
      <View style={styles.container}>
        <Text style={styles.welcome}>
          Welcome to React Native!
        </Text>
        <Text style={styles.instructions}>
          To get started, edit index.ios.js
        </Text>
        <Text style={styles.instructions}>
          Press Cmd+R to reload,{'\n'}
          Cmd+D or shake for dev menu
        </Text>
      </View>
    );
  }
});

var styles = StyleSheet.create({
  container: {
    flex: 1,
    justifyContent: 'center',
    alignItems: 'center',
    backgroundColor: '#F5FCFF',
  },
```

```
  welcome: {
    fontSize: 20,
    textAlign: 'center',
    margin: 10,
  },
  instructions: {
    textAlign: 'center',
    color: '#333333',
    marginBottom: 5,
  },
});

AppRegistry.registerComponent('ReactNotes', () => ReactNotes);
```

 Although `react-native-cli` generates the starter template using the ES5 `createClass`, we will be creating our components using ES6 classes.

A lot of things are included in here, but bear with us as we break it down for you. If we take a closer look at the render method, we can see the familiar `View` and `Text` components that we encountered in the previous chapter. Note how the index file is a component itself (`ReactNotes`). Change the value in line `30` to `Welcome to React Notes!`. Save it and then press *Cmd + R* from the simulator or, in the top menu, navigate to **Hardware | Shake Gesture** and select **Reload** from the pop-up action sheet. The text on screen re-renders to show the text value we just modified! We are no longer constrained to wait for the Xcode to recompile in order to see our changes as we can reload straight from the simulator. Continue making changes and reload it in the simulator to get a feel for the work flow.

Structuring the application

It's time to add a little interactivity to our application. You can begin by adding a simple button component to the screen that is touchable. In the root directory, create a folder called `App` and another folder inside the `App` folder called `Components`. In the `Components` directory, add a file named `SimpleButton.js`. This will be the directory in which we store and reference the components we create.

 Note that the React Native code created in this chapter will work for both iOS and Android. Simply replace `index.ios.js` with `index.android.js` if you are interested in android only. The screenshots and instructions will be mainly for the iOS simulator.

Creating the SimpleButton component

Let's start by rendering some text to the screen and importing it into our `index.ios.js` file. In `SimpleButton.js`, add:

```
import React, {
    Text,
    View
} from 'react-native';

export default class SimpleButton extends React.Component {
  render () {
    return (
      <View>
        <Text>Simple Button</Text>
      </View>
    );
  }
}
```

 ES6 de-structuring assignment `var [a, b] = [1, 2];` is used to extract `Text` and `View` from the React Native module.

We are going to include our newly created component in `index.ios.js` and simplify it to ES6 syntax:

```
import React, {
  AppRegistry,
  StyleSheet,
  View
} from 'react-native';

import SimpleButton from './App/Components/SimpleButton';

class ReactNotes extends React.Component {
  render () {
    return (
      <View style={styles.container}>
        <SimpleButton />
      </View>
    );
  }
}
```

```
var styles = StyleSheet.create({
  container: {
    flex: 1,
    justifyContent: 'center',
    alignItems: 'center',
  }
});
AppRegistry.registerComponent('ReactNotes', () => ReactNotes);
```

The output for the preceding code is:

We're off to a good start; it's time to add some interactivity to our button. In `SimpleButton.js`, add the `TouchableOpacity` component to the destructuring assignment. `TouchableHighlight`, `TouchableOpacity`, and `TouchableWithoutFeedback` are similar components that respond to touches, and it takes an `onPress` prop for a function to react to the touch. Wrap the existing code in the render function with the `TouchableOpacity` component:

```
import React, {
Text,
TouchableOpacity,
View
} from 'react-native';


export default class SimpleButton extends React.Component {
  render () {
    return (
      <TouchableOpacity onPress={() => console.log('Pressed!')}>
        <View>
          <Text>Simple Button</Text>
        </View>
      </TouchableOpacity>
    );
  }
}
```

Go ahead and try tapping (or clicking) on the text now, you should be able to see that the opacity of the text decreases as you press it. But where has our `console.log(...)` output gone? Open the **Developer** menu (**Hardware | Shake Gesture**) and select **Debug** in Chrome. This opens a Chrome Window at `localhost:8081/debugger-ui` for debugging, as shown in the following screenshot:

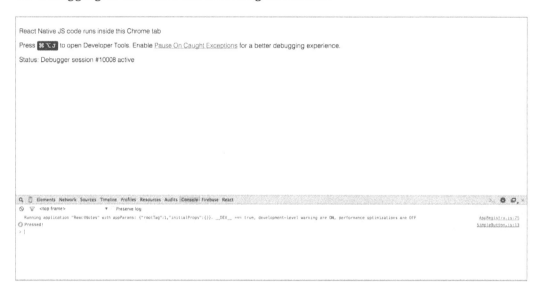

Lo and behold, here is the console log that we specified in our `SimpleButton` component. Behind the scenes, the JavaScript code is being run from inside the Chrome tab and loaded onto the mobile device on startup or reload. From here, you have access to all the Chrome Developer Tools you will normally use, including the addition of break points.

Navigation

Now, its time to make our application more actionable. Let's begin by transforming our `SimpleButton` into a **Create Note** button. When the user clicks on the **Create Note** button, it transitions them to another screen to create notes. To do this, we need our button to be able to accept a function via props from `index.ios.js` to activate the transition. We will add some custom text as well for extra flair:

```
import React, {
Text,
TouchableOpacity,
View
} from 'react-native';
```

```
export default class SimpleButton extends React.Component {
  render () {
    return (
      <TouchableOpacity onPress={this.props.onPress}>
        <View>
          <Text>{this.props.customText || 'Simple Button'}</Text>
        </View>
      </TouchableOpacity>
    );
  }
}

SimpleButton.propTypes = {
  onPress: React.PropTypes.func.isRequired,
  customText: React.PropTypes.string
};
```

Now, we have extended our `SimpleButton` component to be reusable with minimal changes. We can always pass different functions through the `onPress` prop and add custom text if we choose. This is all that we need to modify our `SimpleButton`; now to include the transition functionality to our `index.io.js` file.

The following image shows the validating props revisited page:

 Remember `propTypes` from the previous chapter? If we forget to pass the `onPress` prop, the console will log a warning reminding us to pass it. Note that there is no warning for `customText` since it was not set to `isRequired`.

The Navigator component

The **Navigator** component is a reimplementation of the `UINavigationController` provided by React Native to manage various screens. Similar to a stack, you can push, pop, and replace routes onto the Navigator. It is fully customizable on both iOS and Android, which we will cover in the next chapter. Import the Navigator into index.ios.js and replace the contents of the render method with:

```
import React, {
  AppRegistry,
  Navigator,
  StyleSheet,
  View
} from 'react-native';


render () {
  return (
    <Navigator
      initialRoute={{name: 'home'}}
      renderScene={this.renderScene}
    />
  );
}
```

Navigator receives a prop called `initialRoute` that accepts an object to be the first route to be put on the stack. The route object can contain any attribute that you need to pass to the screen components. All we need for now is the name of the screen we want to transition to. Next, we need to create the `function` to pass to the `renderScene` prop. In the `ReactNotes` component, we are going to create a `function` that takes `route` and `navigator` as parameters, as shown:

```
class ReactNotes extends React.Component {
  renderScene (route, navigator) {
    ...
  }
  render () {
    ...
  }
}
```

When we first load our application, the parameter `route` will be the object we pass into `initialRoute`. Using a switch statement and looking at the values of `route.name` allows us to choose the component we want to render:

```
renderScene (route, navigator) {
  switch (route.name) {
    case 'home':
      return (
        <View style={styles.container}>
          <SimpleButton
            onPress={() => console.log('Pressed!')}
            customText='Create Note'
          />
        </View>
      );
    case 'createNote':
  }
}
```

Here, under the `home` case, you can see our slightly modified code from the original `render` method in `ReactNotes`; we have included the `onPress` and `customText` props we created earlier. You can add another component to `App/Componets/` named `NoteScreen.js`; this screen will contain the functionality to create a new note:

```
import React, {
  StyleSheet,
  Text,
  View
} from 'react-native';

export default class NoteScreen extends React.Component {
  render () {
    return (
      <View style={styles.container}>
        <Text>Create Note Screen!</Text>
      </View>
    );
  }
}

var styles = StyleSheet.create({
  container: {
    flex: 1,
    justifyContent: 'center',
    alignItems: 'center',
  }
});
```

For now, we are only going to use this screen when we press the **Create Note** button. In the `onPress` prop arrow function, we are going to push a new route onto the stack using `navigator.push`:

```
import NoteScreen from './App/Components/NoteScreen';

class ReactNotes extends React.Component {
  renderScene (route, navigator) {
    switch (route.name) {
      case 'home':
        return (
          <View style={styles.container}>
            <SimpleButton
              onPress={() => {
                navigator.push({
                  name: 'createNote'
                });
              }}
              customText='Create Note'
            />
          </View>
        );
      case 'createNote':
        return (
          <NoteScreen />
        );
    }
  }
}
```

Note that push also takes a regular JavaScript object, so we need to include the name attribute for our `NoteScreen`; reload the application in the simulator and press on the **Create Note** button. A smooth animated transition between the two screens will occur without adding any extra code.

Navigator.NavigationBar

At this point you must be thinking *A button is OK, but is there a better, more native way to do navigation?* Of course, as a part of the Navigator component, you can pass a `navigationBar` prop to add a persistent top navigation bar across every screen. The `Navigator.NavigationBar` is a subcomponent that accepts an object that defines the left and right buttons, a title, and styles (although we are going to leave it `unstyled` until the next chapter). Modify the `ReactNotes` render function to include the `navigationBar`, as shown:

```
render () {
  return (
    <Navigator
```

```
      initialRoute={{name: 'home'}}
      renderScene={this.renderScene}
      navigationBar={
        <Navigator.NavigationBar
          routeMapper={NavigationBarRouteMapper}
        />
      }
    />
  );
}
```

The `routeMapper` prop accepts an object containing functions for the `LeftButton`, `RightButton`, and `Title` attributes. Let's insert this object after the imports at the top of `index.ios.js`:

```
var NavigationBarRouteMapper = {
  LeftButton: function(route, navigator, index, navState) {
    ...
  },

  RightButton: function(route, navigator, index, navState) {
    ...
  },

  Title: function(route, navigator, index, navState) {
    ...
  }
};
```

Advancing the flow of our application to the `CreateNote` screen will require displaying a right-hand button in the navigator bar. Luckily, we already have our simple button set up to push the state onto the navigator. In the `RightButton` function, add:

```
var NavigationBarRouteMapper = {
  ...

  RightButton: function(route, navigator, index, navState) {
    switch (route.name) {
      case 'home':
        return (
          <SimpleButton
            onPress={() => {
              navigator.push({
                name: 'createNote'
```

```
          });
        }}
          customText='Create Note'
      />
    );
  default:
    return null;
  }
},


  ...

};
```

Similar to our previous `renderScene` method, we can switch on the value of `route.name`. The default expression in the `switch` statement is there to ensure that different screens do not return a button unless we include them. Let's also go ahead and add a `LeftButton` to the `NavigationBar` when it's on the `NoteScreen` to return to the home screen.

```
var NavigationBarRouteMapper = {
  LeftButton: function(route, navigator, index, navState) {
    switch (route.name) {
      case 'createNote':
        return (
          <SimpleButton
            onPress={() => navigator.pop()}
            customText='Back'
          />
        );
      default:
        return null;
    }
  },


  ...

};
```

The `navigator.pop()` will remove the route on the top of the stack; thus, returning us to our original view. Finally, to add a title, we do the exact same thing in the `Title` attributes function:

```
var NavigationBarRouteMapper = {

  ...

  Title: function(route, navigator, index, navState) {
    switch (route.name) {
```

```
      case 'home':
        return (
          <Text>React Notes</Text>
        );
      case 'createNote':
        return (
          <Text>Create Note</Text>
        );
    }
  }
};
```

Now, let's update the original `renderScene` function to get rid of the button
and include the home screen as a component. Create a new component called
`HomeScreen`; the contents of this screen won't matter much, as we will come
back to it later:

```
import React, {
  StyleSheet,
  Text,
  View
  } from 'react-native';
export default class HomeScreen extends React.Component {
  render () {
    return (
      <View style={styles.container}>
        <Text>Home</Text>
      </View>
    );
  }
}
var styles = StyleSheet.create({
  container: {
    flex: 1,
    justifyContent: 'center',
    alignItems: 'center',
  }
});
```

Then import it into `index.ios.js` or `index.android.js`:

```
import HomeScreen from './App/Components/HomeScreen';

...
```

```
class ReactNotes extends React.Component {
  renderScene (route, navigator) {
    switch (route.name) {
      case 'home':
        return (
          <HomeScreen />
        );
      case 'createNote':
        return (
          <NoteScreen />
        );
    }
  }

  ...

}
```

Now, let's see how the navigation bar persists across each route:

That's it! Reload and take a look at how the static navigation bar persists across each route:

For a more detailed guide on Navigator, check out the React Native documentation at `https://facebook.github.io/react-native/docs/navigator.html`. We now have the proper infrastructure to go ahead and start adding the create note functionality to our application.

The NoteScreen – first pass

Now that we have a NoteScreen and can navigate to it, let's start making it useful. We'll need to add some TextInput components, one for the title of the note and one to capture the body. We'll want to automatically set focus on the TextInput for the title, so the user can start typing right away. We'll need to listen to events on the TextInput components, so we can keep a track of what the user has typed by updating the state. We'd also like to know when the user has finished editing the title of the note, so that we can automatically set focus on the TextInput for the body.

First, let's add the TextInput component to our list of dependencies and remove the Text component since we no longer need it:

```
import React, {
  StyleSheet,
  TextInput,
  View
}from 'react-native';
```

Before we add the TextInput components to the View, let's get a few style updates out of the way:

```
var styles = StyleSheet.create({
  container: {
    flex: 1,
    justifyContent: 'center',
    alignItems: 'center',
    marginTop: 64
  },
  title: {
    height: 40
  },
  body: {
    flex: 1
  }
});
```

Note that we've added a marginTop: 64 to the container. This is important because we want to make sure that the NavigationBar doesn't accidentally intercept the onPress events we want our TextInput to receive. We've also added styles for each of the TextInputs we're about to add. We'll talk more about styles in detail in *Chapter 4, Working with Styles and Layout*.

Now, in our render function, let's replace the `Text` component with two `TextInput` components, such as:

```
render () {
  return (
    <View style={styles.container}>
      <TextInput placeholder="Untitled"
        style={styles.title}/>
      <TextInput multiline={true}
      placeholder="Start typing" style={styles.body}/>
    </View>
  );
}
```

Before we try this out, notice that the `TextInput` component has a placeholder property that allows us to tell the user what the `TextInput` is for without having to take up additional screen real estate by labeling our form fields. I've also specified `multiline={true}` on the second `TextInput` so the user can add as much text as they want.

Now let's refresh the application in the simulator and you should see something like this:

You should be able to click into `TextInput` and start typing. If you'd like to use the on-screen keyboard available in the simulator, you can press *Cmd+K / Ctrl+K.*

Let's improve the user experience a little bit by making the title `TextInput` focus automatically and show the keyboard when the user navigates to the `NoteScreen`:

```
<TextInput
  ref="title"
  autoFocus={true}
  placeholder="Untitled"
 style={styles.title}
/>
```

To be even more user friendly, let's listen for the event that tells us the user has finished editing the title and automatically set focus on the body `TextInput`. To do that we'll need to make a slight change to the body `TextInput` so that we can refer to it in our event handler:

```
<TextInput
  ref="body"
  multiline={true}
  placeholder="Start typing"
  style={styles.body}
/>
```

Notice the `ref="body"`. Any React component can be given a `ref` so that it can be referenced in your `javascript` code. Now, in the title `TextInput`, we can add an `onEndEditing` event handler that sets focus on the `TextInput` body:

```
<TextInput
  autoFocus={true}
  placeholder="Untitled"
  style={styles.title}
  onEndEditing={ (text) => {this.refs.body.focus()}}
/>
```

 Avoid using refs to set and get values on your components! That's what `state` is for and we'll learn all about state in *Chapter 5, Displaying and Saving Data.*

Now when you refresh the application in the simulator and navigate to the `NoteScreen`, you will see that the title `TextInput` has focus and you should be able to type something. Press *Enter* and see the focus automatically switch to the body and start typing there as well. If you're not seeing the on-screen keyboard when you try this, press *Cmd + K / Ctrl + K* and try again.

Summary

In this chapter, we have created the skeleton of our ReactNotes application, walked you through how to create a new project, created Views and custom components, navigated between the HomeScreen and NoteScreen, and debugged your application.

You now have a solid foundation for all of the topics we'll introduce throughout the rest of the book. However, there are two big problems with this application, it's not pretty and it doesn't do anything! In the next two chapters, we'll solve both of those problems and you'll be well on your way to master React Native!

4
Working with Styles and Layout

At this point, you may feel that the application is lacking a certain appeal. The success of any application relies greatly on how the user interface looks. Just like how React Native borrows from React on the web, the same thing goes for styles. In this chapter, you will learn how React Native styles and lays out the components with React CSS.

We will cover the following topics:

- What is React CSS?
- Creating Style Sheets
- Extending the `SimpleButton` to include custom styles
- An introduction to layout with Flexbox
- Styling the `NavigationBar`
- Styling the `NoteScreen`

React CSS

If you have any experience in writing CSS for a browser then you will feel comfortable with the styles in React Native. Although, instead of the browser's implementation of cascading styles, Facebook has developed a subset version of CSS in JavaScript. The benefit of this approach is that the designer can fully utilize features in JavaScript, such as variables and conditionals, which CSS does not support natively.

Style Sheet

Style Sheet is the React Native abstraction to declare styles using object notation. The components can use any style, so if you find that you are not able to get the right look then refer to the React Native documentation on that component in its styles section.

When inserting styles, it is common to include only those styles that you need for that specific component. It is similar to how JSX combines the JavaScript logic and markup into a single component; we are also going to define our styles in the same file.

To create a Style Sheet, use the `Stylesheet.create({..})` method by passing in an object of objects:

```
var styles = StyleSheet.create({
  myStyle: {
    backgroundColor: '#EEEEEE'
    color: 'black'
  }
});
```

This looks similar to CSS but it uses commas instead of semicolons.

Styles are declared to be *inline* on a component using the style prop:

```
// Using StyleSheet
<Component style={styles.myStyle} />
// Object
<Component style={{color: 'white'}} />
```

It is also possible to pass normal JavaScript objects to the style prop. This is generally not recommended, since the Style Sheet ensures that each style is immutable and only created once throughout the lifecycle.

Styling the SimpleButton component

Let's extend our `SimpleButton` component further to accept custom styles for the button background and text. In the `render` method, let's set the `style` attribute of the `View` and `Text` components from the `props`:

```
export default class SimpleButton extends React.Component {
  render () {
    return (
      <TouchableOpacity onPress={this.props.onPress}>
        <View style={this.props.style}>
```

```
        <Text style={this.props.textStyle}>
          {this.props.customText || 'Simple Button'}
        </Text>
      </View>
    </TouchableOpacity>
  );
  }
}

SimpleButton.propTypes = {
    onPress: React.PropTypes.func.isRequired,
    customText: React.PropTypes.string,
    style: View.propTypes.style,
    textStyle: Text.propTypes.style
};
```

Revisiting PropTypes

To validate, the View or Text styles passed into your component use View.propTypes.style and Text.propType.style.

On the HomeScreen we are going to style the simpleButton component to draw the user's attention to the NoteScreen when there are no notes. We will start by adding it to the StyleSheet and defining some text styles:

```
var styles = StyleSheet.create({
  ...

  simpleButtonText: {
    color: 'white',
    fontWeight: 'bold',
    fontSize: 16
  }
});
```

Here, we want the text on the button to be bold, white in color, and with size 16. To style the button, we need to add another object to the StyleSheet called simpleButton and also define a background color; the simpleButton code is as follows:

```
var styles = StyleSheet.create({
  ...

  simpleButton: {
```

```
      backgroundColor: '#5B29C1',
    },
    simpleButtonText: {
      color: 'white',
      fontWeight: 'bold',
      fontSize: 16
    }
  });
```

Let's see the output of the preceding command:

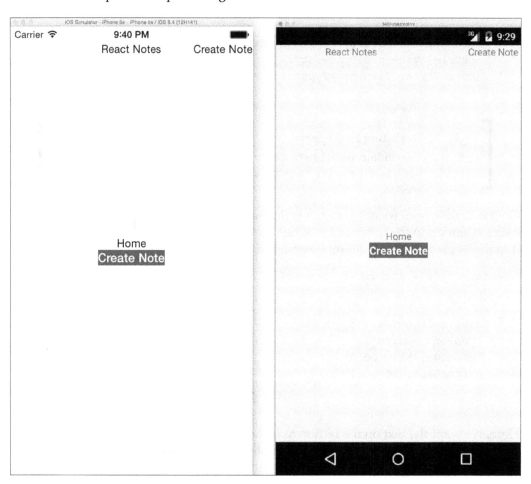

It's not that appealing yet; let's add some padding so that it's easier for the user to press the button:

```
paddingHorizontal: 20,
paddingVertical: 15,
```

paddingVertical is shorthand for paddingTop and paddingBottom. paddingHorizontal is shorthand for paddingLeft and paddingRight.

React CSS does not have a shorthand notion, such as border: 1px solid #000. Instead each item is declared individually:

```
borderColor: '#48209A',
borderWidth: 1,
borderRadius: 4,
```

To add a drop shadow, we define each property similar to borders:

```
shadowColor: 'darkgrey',
    shadowOffset: {
        width: 1,
        height: 1
    },
    shadowOpacity: 0.8,
    shadowRadius: 1,
```

Notice how the shadow offset requires an object with width and height properties. Since we are dealing with JavaScript objects, this is a perfectly acceptable notation. Now, we include the SimpleButton component in our HomeScreen render method:

```
...
import SimpleButton from './SimpleButton';

export default class HomeScreen extends React.Component {
  render () {
    return (
      <View style={styles.container}>
        <Text style={styles.noNotesText}>You haven't created any
notes!</Text>

        <SimpleButton
          onPress={() => this.props.navigator.push({
            name: 'createNote'
          })}
          customText="Create Note"
          style={styles.simpleButton}
          textStyle={styles.simpleButtonText}
        />
      </View>
    );
```

```
      }
    }

    var styles = StyleSheet.create({
      container: {
        flex: 1,
        justifyContent: 'center',
        alignItems: 'center',
      },
      noNotesText: {
        color: '#48209A',
        marginBottom: 10
      },
      simpleButton: {
        backgroundColor: '#5B29C1',
        borderColor: '#48209A',
        borderWidth: 1,
        borderRadius: 4,
        paddingHorizontal: 20,
        paddingVertical: 15,
        shadowColor: 'darkgrey',
        shadowOffset: {
            width: 1,
            height: 1
        },
        shadowOpacity: 0.8,
        shadowRadius: 1,
      },
      simpleButtonText: {
        color: 'white',
        fontWeight: 'bold',
        fontSize: 16
      }
    });
```

Update the `renderScene` function of `ReactNotes` in `index.ios.js` and `index.android.js` to pass the navigator through the `props` to the `HomeScreen`:

```
class ReactNotes extends React.Component {
  renderScene (route, navigator) {
    switch (route.name) {
      case 'home':
        return (
          <HomeScreen navigator={navigator} />
        );
```

```
      case 'createNote':
        return (
          <NoteScreen />
        );
    }
  }

  ...

}
```

Let's see the output of the preceding command:

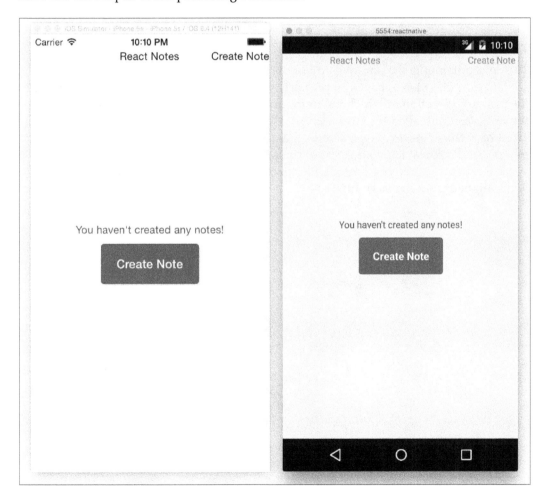

This is not too shabby for a typical call to action button. If you reload this in the simulator and press the button, it will still fade due to the `TouchableOpacity` feedback. For more information on React CSS or to contribute, visit the open source CSS-layout repository at `https://github.com/facebook/css-layout`.

Layout and Flexbox

Since Flexbox is the foundation of React Native's layout, we are going to explore it in depth. If you are already familiar with the intricacies of Flexbox, feel free to jump to the *Styling the NavigationBar component* section. There we will focus more on the styling of the components that we made in the previous chapter.

Flex container

The flex container is the parent element that describes how children or flex items are laid out. The `flexDirection` property of the container specifies the `main-axis`; the primary direction in which the items are rendered. The line perpendicular to the `main-axis` is called the `cross-axis`. Different flex properties on the container affect how the items are aligned across each axis. The `flexDirection` property has two possible values; `row` values for horizontal layouts (left to right) and `column` for vertical layouts (top to bottom). The following figure shows the `flexDirection: row` items aligned from left to right:

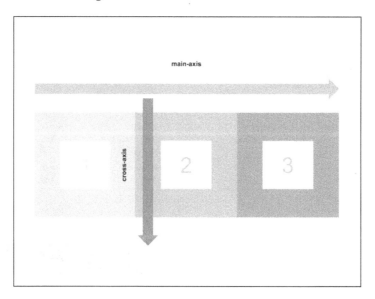

The next figure shows the items laid out from top to bottom when it's set to `flexDirection: column`:

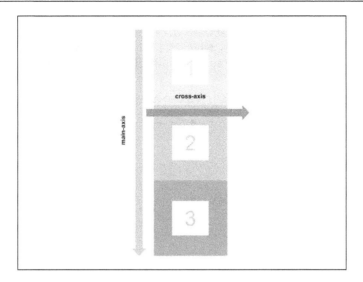

We can move the items in the container along the established main-axis with the help of justifyContent. The following diagram shows the different options along the main-axis:

Notice how `space-between` does not include white space along the left and right edges, whereas `space-around` does, but it is half the width of the white space included in between the items.

To move items along the `cross-axis`, we use `alignItems`:

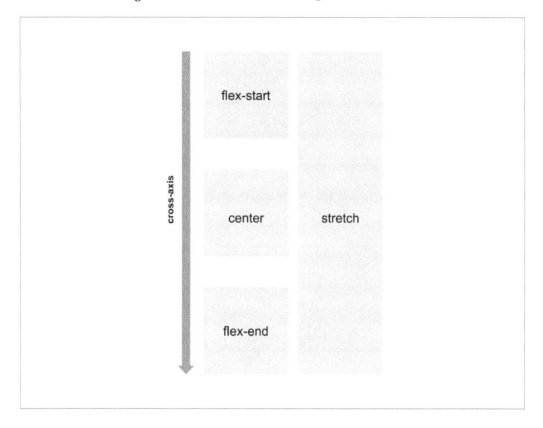

Wrapping items is also possible, but it is disabled by default. Items within a container will all try to fit along the `main-axis`. If there are too many items or if they are too squeezed, you can apply `flexWrap`. The container will then calculate if it is necessary to put an item onto a new row or column.

Flex items

By default, `flex` items will only be as wide as their internal content. The `flex` property dictates the amount of remaining space the item should take up. The available space is divided based on the ratio of each item's `flex` value:

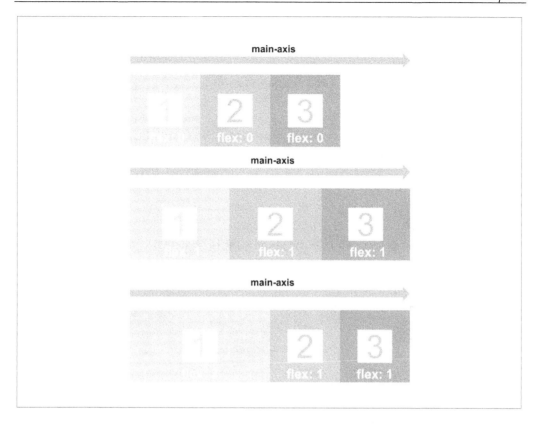

Make a note of how the items in row two are all of the same width, since their `flex` value is `1`. The item with `flex` value `2` in row three takes twice as much space as the rest of the items.

Similar to `alignItems`, a `flex` item can align itself along the `cross-axis` with `alignSelf`.

Horizontal and vertical centering

Let's take a look at a quick example of how Flexbox makes layout easier. One of the biggest challenges in CSS is the vertically and horizontally centered elements (take five minutes and attempt to accomplish this in normal CSS). We're going to start by creating our `Center` components and defining a `flex` container with three `flex` items:

```
class Center extends React.Component {
    render () {
        return (
            <View style={styles.container}>
```

```
                    <View style={[styles.item, styles.one]}>
                        <Text style={styles.itemText}>1</Text>
                    </View>
                    <View style={[styles.item, styles.two]}>
                        <Text style={styles.itemText}>2</Text>
                    </View>
                    <View style={[styles.item, styles.three]}>
                        <Text style={styles.itemText}>3</Text>
                    </View>
                </View>
            );
        }
    }
```

Initialize a new StyleSheet and define some simple styles for the items:

```
    var styles = StyleSheet.create({
      item: {
        backgroundColor: '#EEE',
        padding: 25
      },
      one: {
        backgroundColor: 'red'
      },
      two: {
        backgroundColor: 'green'
      },
      three: {
        backgroundColor: 'blue'
      },
      itemText: {
        color: 'white',
        fontSize: 40,
      }
    });
```

Now, we want to control where the items are aligned along the `main-axis` and `cross-axis` with `justifyContent` and `alignItems`. Create a container style and set `justifyContent` and align items to `center`:

```
var styles = StyleSheet.create({
  container: {
    flexDirection: 'row',
    alignItems: 'center',
    justifyContent: 'center'
  },

  ...
});
```

This does not seem like the behaviour was specified. The items are aligned along the centre of the main-axis but not the cross-axis. Let's add a border around the container to visualize it:

```
var styles = StyleSheet.create({
  container: {
    borderWidth: 10,
    borderColor: 'purple',
    flexDirection: 'row',
    alignItems: 'center',
    justifyContent: 'center'
  },

  . . .
});
```

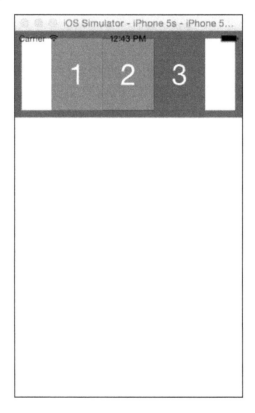

Now we can see that the height of the container does not span the entire screen. Since the default flexDirection in the root View container is column, the content will only span the height of the content. Luckily, we now know the property to take up the remaining space. Adding flex 1 to our container will have its span in the vertical length of the screen, which gives us the following:

```
var styles = StyleSheet.create({
  container: {
    borderWidth: 10,
    borderColor: 'purple',
    flex: 1,
    flexDirection: 'row',
    alignItems: 'center',
    justifyContent: 'center'
  },

  ...
});
```

This completes our overview of layout with Flexbox! For the entire list of supported Flexbox properties, check out the React Native documentation at `https://facebook.github.io/react-native/docs/flexbox.html#content`.

Absolute positioning

Additionally, React Native gives you the option of positioning the items on your screen. This works the same way as it does in the browser by defining the `top`, `left`, `right`, and `bottom` properties. We recommend that you try to create your layout in Flexbox before resorting to absolute positioning.

Styling the NavigationBar component

It's time to give our `NavigationBar` the iOS and Android style treatment. There is a small difference between the two, except for how the font size and padding are rendered. We will start by giving our `NavigationBar` a background color and a bottom border. Add this to the `StyleSheet` in `index.ios.js` and `index.android.js` and define the `navbar` style:

```
var styles = StyleSheet.create({
    navContainer: {
      flex: 1
    },
    navBar: {
      backgroundColor: '#5B29C1',
      borderBottomColor: '#48209A',
      borderBottomWidth: 1
    }
});
```

Next, update the `Navigator.NavigatorBar` with the style prop:

```
class ReactNotes extends React.Component {
  ...
  render () {
    return (
      <Navigator
        initialRoute={{name: 'home'}}
        renderScene={this.renderScene}
        navigationBar={
          <Navigator.NavigationBar
            routeMapper={NavigationBarRouteMapper}
            style={styles.navBar}
          />
```

```
            }
        />
    );
  }
}
```

The last things to be updated are our `navbar` title and `SimpleButton` styles. We want the text to be `centered` vertically as well as to give the left-hand and right-hand buttons some padding from the sides of the screen:

```
var styles = StyleSheet.create({
    navBar: {
        backgroundColor: '#5B29C1',
        borderBottomColor: '#48209A',
        borderBottomWidth: 1
    },
    navBarTitleText: {
        color: 'white',
        fontSize: 16,
        fontWeight: '500',
        marginVertical: 9  // iOS
// marginVertical: 16 // Android
    },
    navBarLeftButton: {
        paddingLeft: 10
    },
    navBarRightButton: {
        paddingRight: 10
    },
    navBarButtonText: {
        color: '#EEE',
        fontSize: 16,
        marginVertical: 10 // iOS
// marginVertical: 16 // Android
    }
});
```

 As we alluded to earlier, the `marginVertical` for iOS is different than the Android version to produce the same visual result.

Finally, update the `NavigationBarRouteMapper` to include the styles for the title and buttons:

```
var NavigationBarRouteMapper = {
  LeftButton: function(route, navigator, index, navState) {
    switch (route.name) {
      case 'createNote':
        return (
          <SimpleButton
            onPress={() => navigator.pop()}
            customText='Back'
            style={styles.navBarLeftButton}
            textStyle={styles.navBarButtonText}
          />
        );
      default:
        return null;
    }
  },
  RightButton: function(route, navigator, index, navState) {
    switch (route.name) {
      case 'home':
        return (
          <SimpleButton
            onPress={() => {
              navigator.push({
                name: 'createNote'
              });
            }}
            customText='Create Note'
            style={styles.navBarRightButton}
            textStyle={styles.navBarButtonText}
          />
        );
      default:
        return null;
    }
  },

  Title: function(route, navigator, index, navState) {
    switch (route.name) {
      case 'home':
        return (
```

```
      <Text style={styles.navBarTitleText}>React Notes</Text>
    );
  case 'createNote':
    return (
      <Text style={styles.navBarTitleText}>Create Note</Text>
    );
  }
 }
};
```

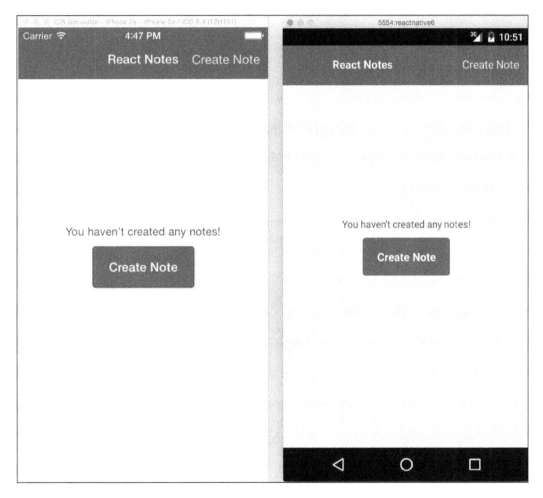

Make a note of how the iOS version, for which we have changed the status bar text to appear white. React Native provides an API to interact with the status bar in iOS. In our index.ios.js we can toggle it to white in the ReactNotes constructor:

```
class ReactNotes extends React.Component {
  constructor (props) {
    super(props);
    StatusBarIOS.setStyle('light-content');
  }
  ...
}
```

The documentation for StatusBarIOS can be found in the React Native documentation at https://facebook.github.io/react-native/docs/statusbarios.html.

Changing the Android Material Theme

The color of the status and navigation bar on our Android application appears to be solid black. Currently, there is no support system in React Native to style these from JavaScript like what the StatusBarIOS API provides on iOS. We can still use the Material Theme (available in Android 5.0 and above), located in ReactNotes/android/app/src/6main/res/values/styles.xml, to apply the colors we want. Change the contents of styles.xml to the following:

```
<resources>
    <!-- Base application theme. -->
    <style name="AppTheme"
      parent="Theme.AppCompat.Light.NoActionBar">
        <item name="android:colorPrimaryDark">#48209A</item>
        <item name="android:navigationBarColor">#48209A</item>
    </style>
</resources>
```

The colorPrimaryDark refers to the color of the status bar, whereas navigationBarColor is the color of the bottom navigation container. When you re-launch the application you should be able to see the status and navigation bars colored correctly.

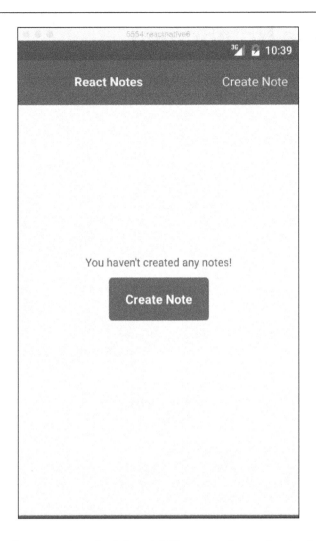

For more information on using the Material Theme, refer to the Android developers documentation at `https://developer.android.com/training/material/theme.html`.

Styling the NoteScreen

Our `NoteScreen` has two `TextInput`s without any styles. As of right now, it's difficult to see where each input rests on the screen. It is common on iOS and Android to put an underline under each input. To achieve this, we are going to wrap our `TextInput` in `View` and apply `borderBottom` to it:

```
var styles = StyleSheet.create({
  ...

  inputContainer: {
    borderBottomColor: '#9E7CE3',
    borderBottomWidth: 1,
    flexDirection: 'row',
    marginBottom: 10
  }
});
```

Apply the inputContainer style to Views:

```
export default class NoteScreen extends React.Component {
  render () {
    return (
      <View style={styles.container}>
        <View style={styles.inputContainer}>
          <TextInput
            autoFocus={true}
            autoCapitalize="sentences"
            placeholder="Untitled"
            style={styles.title}

            onEndEditing={(text) => {this.refs.body.focus()}}
          />
        </View>
        <View style={styles.inputContainer}>
          <TextInput
            ref="body"
            multiline={true}
            placeholder="Start typing"
            style={styles.body}
```

```
                textAlignVertical="top"
                underlineColorAndroid="transparent"
              />
           </View>
         </View>
       );
     }
   }
```

The existing title and body styles define the height of each `TextInput`. Since each input will share the `flex` properties and text size, we can define a shared style:

```
var styles = StyleSheet.create({
  ...
  textInput: {
    flex: 1,
    fontSize: 16,
  },

});
```

Then, in each input style we can pass an array to include both styles:

```
class NoteScreen extends React.Component {
  render () {
    return (
      <View style={styles.container}>
        <View style={styles.inputContainer}>
          <TextInput
            autoFocus={true}
            autoCapitalize="sentences"
            placeholder="Untitled"
            style={[styles.textInput, styles.title]}
            onEndEditing={(text) => {this.refs.body.focus()}}
          />
        </View>
        <View style={styles.inputContainer}>
          <TextInput
            ref="body"
            multiline={true}
            placeholder="Start typing"
            style={[styles.textInput, styles.body]}
          />
```

```
          </View>
        </View>
    );
  }
}
```

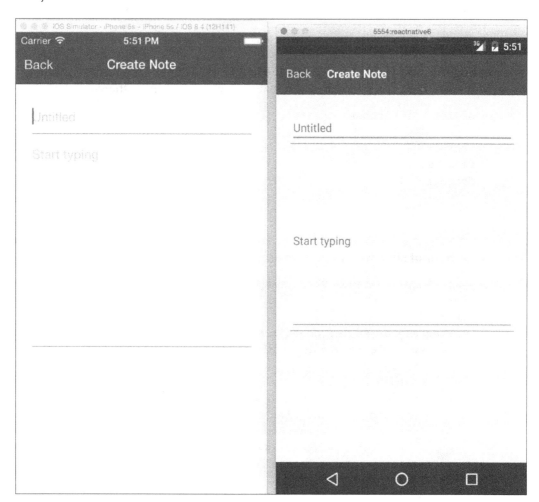

This doesn't look right on Android yet. The TextInputs on Android have a default underline and they center the text vertically on multiline inputs. There are two Android only attributes that can be added to match the look of the iOS application. On each TextInput set the underlineColorAndroid as transparent and textAlignVertical on the body as TextInput:

```
export default class NoteScreen extends React.Component {
  render () {
    return (
      <View style={styles.container}>
        <View style={styles.inputContainer}>
          <TextInput
            autoFocus={true}
            autoCapitalize="sentences"
            placeholder="Untitled"
            style={[styles.textInput, styles.title]}
            onEndEditing={(text) => {this.refs.body.focus()}}
            underlineColorAndroid="transparent"
          />
        </View>
        <View style={styles.inputContainer}>
          <TextInput
            ref="body"
            multiline={true}
            placeholder="Start typing"
            style={[styles.textInput, styles.body]}
            textAlignVertical="top"
            underlineColorAndroid="transparent"
          />
        </View>
```

```
        </View>
    );
  }
}
```

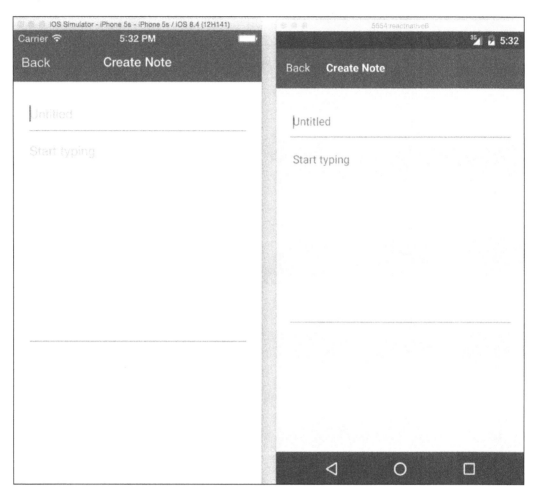

With this we get the same look on both devices! This wraps up the styling of the components we created in the previous chapter. Henceforth, we are going to style as soon as we add new components to our application.

Summary

Styles in React Native are very similar to how CSS works in browser. In this chapter, you learned how to create and manage Style Sheets and add them to your components. If you ever find yourself frustrated with the layout then use the Flexbox section as a guide. Make sure to review where your `main-axis` and `cross-axis` are defined, as well as where the `flex` items are aligned along them. Feel free to go back to our components and play around with any of the styles before continuing with the next chapter.

5
Displaying and Saving Data

Now that we know how to style a React Native application, let's figure out how to actually make it do something. In this chapter, we'll start saving notes to the device, populate a list with the notes we've saved, and select notes from the list to view and edit.

In this chapter, we will cover the following topics:

*   Using a `ListView` to display rows of data
*   Managing state
*   Using props to pass data and callbacks into components
*   Using `AsyncStorage` to store data on both iOS and Android devices

Our strategy in this chapter is to first build the basic functionality using dummy data so we can learn some fundamental skills before we learn about saving and loading the data with the `AsyncStorage` API. By the end of the chapter, you will have a fully functional note-taking application!

Lists

The `HomeScreen` of our application is going to display a list of the notes that we have saved. To do this, we will introduce the `ListView` component. Let's start by creating a new file in our `Components` directory called `NoteList` and add the following code:

```
import React, {
  StyleSheet,
  Text,
  View,
  ListView
  } from 'react-native';
```

```
export default class NoteList extends React.Component {

  constructor (props) {
    super(props);
    this.ds = new ListView.DataSource({rowHasChanged: (r1, r2) => r1
!== r2});
  }

  render() {
    return (
      <ListView
        dataSource={
          this.ds.cloneWithRows( [
              {title:"Note 1", body:"Body 1", id:1},
              {title:"Note 2", body:"Body 2", id:2}
            ])
        }
        renderRow={(rowData) => {
            return (
                <Text>{rowData.title}</Text>
            )
          }
        }/>
      )
  }
}
```

The ListView component is fairly simple to use. You must provide two pieces of information, the dataSource that will provide the data for all of the rows and the renderRow function, which is simply a function that takes each row's data (a single note) and returns a React component. In the preceding example, this function returns a <Text/> component that displays the title of the note.

We instantiate a ListView. The DataSource is in the constructor because we only want to create it once. The DataSource constructor takes a params object to configure the DataSource; however, the only required parameter is a rowHasChanged function. This function is used by the DataSource when it receives new data so that it can efficiently determine which rows need to be re-rendered. If r1 and r2 point to the same object, the row hasn't changed.

You'll also notice that we don't pass the DataSource reference directly to our ListView. Instead we use cloneWithRows(), passing it to the rowData we want to use. We're hardcoding the row data for now, but by the end of this chapter you will know how to update the ListView with new data.

Next, let's add the `NoteList` component to the `HomeScreen` and learn how to respond to touch events on each row. Open the `HomeScreen` component and add the following line to import your new `NoteList` component:

```
import NoteList from './NoteList';
```

Also, let's drop the `NoteList` component into `HomeScreen`'s render method just inside the `View` component, before the `<Text/>` component:

```
render () {
    return (
      <View style={styles.container}>
        <NoteList/>
        <Text style={styles.noNotesText}>You haven't created any
notes!</Text>

        <SimpleButton
          onPress={() => this.props.navigator.push({
            name: 'createNote'
          })}
          customText="Create Note"
          style={styles.simpleButton}
          textStyle={styles.simpleButtonText}
        />
      </View>
    );
}
```

Before we try out our `NoteList`, let's modify our styles to make sure that the list content isn't obscured by the `NavigationBar`:

```
container: {
  flex: 1,
  justifyContent: 'center',
  alignItems: 'center',
  marginTop: 60
}
```

Now, when you reload the application you should see the following screenshot:

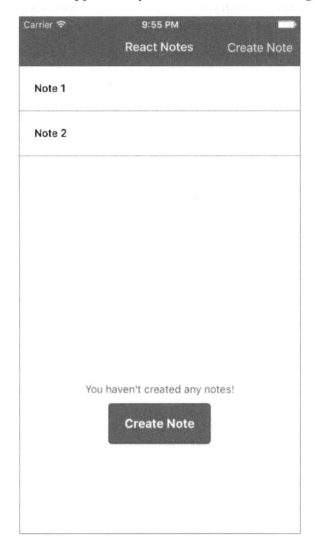

We still have the **You haven't created any notes!** Message at the bottom of the screen, but we'll learn how to take care of that later in the chapter.

Now that we have a list of items, we'd like to be able to respond when the user touches one of the items. To do that, we'll wrap the <Text/> component in our renderRow function with the TouchableHighlight component. First, let's add TouchableHighlight to our list of imports:

```
import React, {
   StyleSheet,
```

```
    Text,
    View,
    ListView,
    TouchableHighlight
    } from 'react-native';
```

Then update the `renderRow` function in our `ListView`:

```
renderRow={
  (rowData) => {
    return (
      <TouchableHighlight onPress={() => console.log(rowData)}>
        <Text>{rowData.title}</Text>
      </TouchableHighlight>
    )
  }
}
```

Now, you can reload the application and touch each row to see that the `rowData` has been logged to the console.

Our goal is to be able to touch a row, navigate to the `NoteScreen`, and populate the title and body with the data from the row. Let's add an `_onPress` event handler to our `NoteList` component, as shown:

```
_onPress (rowData) {
  this.props.navigator.push(
    {
      name: 'createNote',
      note: {
        id: rowData.id,
        title: rowData.title,
        body: rowData.body
      }
    });
}
```

And we will call this function from our `TouchableHighlight`, as shown:

```
              <TouchableHighlight onPress={() =>
                this._onPress(rowData)}>
                <Text>{rowData.title}</Text>
              </TouchableHighlight>
```

Before we try this out, take a look at the `_onPress` handler and notice that we are referring to `this.props.navigator`. This is the navigator that we've been using to go back and forth between the `HomeScreen` and the `NoteScreen`, but what's this props business?

Understanding props

If you take a look at the constructor function of the `NoteList`, you will notice that it takes an argument called **props**:

```
export default class NoteList extends React.Component {
  constructor (props) {
    super(props);
    this.ds = new ListView.DataSource({rowHasChanged: (r1, r2) =>
      r1 !== r2});
  }
}
```

Props is the mechanism we use to pass data to React components. In our case, we want to pass a navigator reference from the `HomeScreen` component to the `NoteList`, so let's make a quick change to our `NoteList` declaration, as shown:

```
export default class HomeScreen extends React.Component {
  render () {
    return (
      <View style={styles.container}>
        <NoteList navigator={this.props.navigator}/>
        ...
      </View>
    );
  }
}
```

When you touch a row in the `NoteList`, you push the note data associated with that row to the navigator, which then triggers `renderScene` that passes the note to the `NoteScreen`. So how do we use this note inside the `NoteScreen`? We learned earlier that props are passed into the component's constructor, but how do we actually get our `TextInput` components to display the note's title and body? Let's see what happens if we bind the value property of each of our inputs to the passed-in note, as shown:

```
<View style={styles.inputContainer}>
  <TextInput
    autoFocus={true}
    autoCapitalize="sentences"
    placeholder="Untitled"
    style={[styles.textInput, styles.title]}
    onEndEditing={(text) => {this.refs.body.focus()}}
    underlineColorAndroid="transparent"
    value={this.props.note.title}
  />
</View>
<View style={styles.inputContainer}>
```

```
<TextInput
  ref="body"
  multiline={true}
  placeholder="Start typing"
  style={[styles.textInput, styles.body]}
  textAlignVertical="top"
  underlineColorAndroid="transparent"
  value={this.props.note.body}
/>
</View>
```

Now when we reload the application and touch the first note in the list, we will see the following screenshot:

But what happens when you try to edit the title or body? Nothing happens! Before we diagnose what is wrong, let's tap the **Back** button and touch the second note in the NoteList. You will see it displayed, as shown:

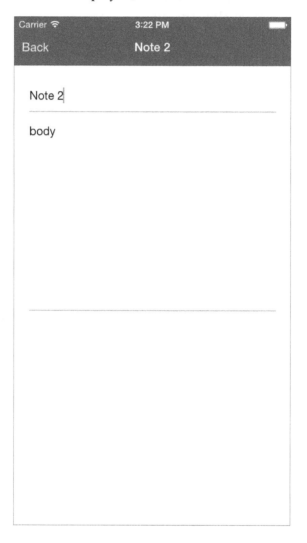

Ok, so our NoteScreen does update, but only when we pass it new props from outside, not when we try to edit the TextInputs. Props can only be passed from the outside of a component. As tempting as it may seem, it's a bad idea to try to modify this.props.note from inside the NoteScreen when the value of each TextInput changes. What we need instead is some way to manage the changes made to the internal state of our NoteScreen when the user makes changes to the TextInputs. For that, each React component has something called **state**.

Using state

React components have a built-in variable called `state` that you can use to keep track of the component's `state`. In the preceding example, we know that we are passing in a note that we want to display, so the initial state of the component is represented by that note. Let's do something totally crazy and modify the `NoteScreen` constructor, as shown:

```
constructor (props) {
  super(props)
  this.state = {note:this.props.note};
}
```

So, `this.state` is an object with title and body properties that are initially set to the title and body of the note we passed. Why the call to *super (props)*? The superclass of our `NoteScreen` is `React.Component`, which takes props as an argument and sets `this.props`. If we omit `super(props)` in `NoteScreen`, then `this.props` will be undefined.

You may have already guessed that we're going to update the `TextInputs` to bind to `this.state.title` and `this.state.body` respectively, but we're also going to listen for `onChangeText` events for each input:

```
<View style={styles.inputContainer}>
  <TextInput
    ref="title"
    autoFocus={true}
    autoCapitalize="sentences"
    placeholder="Untitled"
    style={[styles.textInput, styles.title]}
    onEndEditing={(text) => {this.refs.body.focus()}}
    underlineColorAndroid="transparent"
    value={this.state.note.title}
    onChangeText={(title) => {this.setState({title})}}
  />
</View>
<View style={styles.inputContainer}>
  <TextInput
    ref="body"
    multiline={true}
    placeholder="Start typing"
    style={[styles.textInput, styles.body]}
    textAlignVertical="top"
    underlineColorAndroid="transparent"
    value={this.state.body}
    onChangeText={(body) => {this.setState({body})}}
  />
</View>
```

Note that the `arrow` function that we're using to handle the `onChangeText` event is calling `this.setState(...)` instead of directly setting `this.state.title`. This is an important thing to remember. Anytime you modify state you must use `this.setState()` so that React knows that your component needs to be re-rendered. For performance reasons, calling `setState()` doesn't immediately update `this.state`, so don't let that trip you up!

Reload the application, touch **Note 1** in the list and then change the title to **My note**:

The `TextInput` attribute now reflects the value of `this.state.title` on every call to `render()`, which happens after every call to `this.setState({title})`. So far so good, but what do you think we will see when we navigate back to the `HomeScreen`? Tap the **Back** button and take a look — the title of the first note is still **Note 1** instead of **My note**. Now, when you click on **Note 1** to go back to the `NoteScreen` you'll see that your changes have disappeared. Let's fix this!

We've just identified the need to update our `ListView` when a note is changed. We know that the internal state of the `NoteScreen` changes when we type into the `TextInput` components, but how do we communicate these changes to the rest of the application?

Passing callbacks in props

A common pattern in React is to pass a callback to a component via props. In our case, we want to pass a callback to our `NoteScreen` so that it can let us know when the note is changed. Let's return to the `ReactNotes` component in our `index.ios.js` or `index.android.js` file and update our `renderScene` function, as shown:

```
renderScene (route, navigator) {
  switch (route.name) {
    case 'home':
      return (
        <HomeScreen navigator={navigator} />
      );
    case 'createNote':
      return (
        <NoteScreen
          note={route.note}
          onChangeNote={(note) => console.log("note changed",
            note)}/>
      );
  }
}
```

Here, we are defining a prop called `onChangeNote` and setting its value to an arrow function that will be called when we invoke `onChangeNote` inside our `NoteScreen` component. So, somewhere inside our `NoteScreen` code we're going to add the following line:

```
this.props.onChangeNote(note);
```

Let's revisit the `NoteScreen` and a function to handle the updating of notes:

```
class NoteScreen extends React.Component {
  ...
  updateNote(title, body) {
    var note = Object.assign(this.state.note, {title:title,
body:body});
    this.props.onChangeNote(note);
    this.setState(note);
  }
  ...
}
```

In our title `TextInput`, update the `onChangeText` function, as shown:

```
onChangeText={(title) => this.updateNote(title, this.state.note.body)}
```

And in the body `TextInput`:

```
onChangeText={(body) => this.updateNote(this.state.note.title, body)}
```

Now let's reload our application, touch **Note 1**, and start making changes. If you look at the console you should see each change being logged:

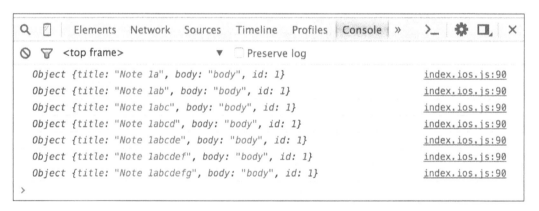

Getting notified of the changes to a note only gets us halfway to our goal to update the `ListView`. Recall that our `NoteList` component's `dataSource` is currently just a hardcoded array of notes:

```
<ListView
    dataSource={
      this.ds.cloneWithRows([
        { title:"Note 1", body:"body", id:1},
        {title:"Note 2", body:"body", id:2}
      ])
```

```
          }
          renderRow={(rowData) => {
              return (
                <TouchableHighlight onPress={() =>
                  this._onPress(rowData)}>
                  <Text>{rowData.title}</Text>
                </TouchableHighlight>
              )
            }
          }
      />
```

We need to be able to pass in the list of notes to the NoteList component instead of hardcoding them. Now that you're familiar with props, you know that we can pass the list in from the HomeScreen, as shown:

```
export default class HomeScreen extends React.Component {
  render () {
    return (
      <View style={styles.container}>
        <NoteList
          navigator={this.props.navigator}
          notes={[{title:"Note 1", body:"body", id:1},
            {title:"Note 2", body:"body", id:2}]}
        />
    ...
  }
```

Then modify the NoteList component to use this.props.notes in the dataSource:

```
export default class NoteList extends React.Component {
...
  render() {
    return (
      <ListView
        dataSource={this.ds.cloneWithRows(this.props.notes)}
        ...
      />
    )
  }
}
```

Let's take our refactoring one step further. We don't really want the HomeScreen to be responsible for managing the state of our list of notes, that's a job for our top-level component, ReactNotes. We can repeat the same trick we just used and replace the hardcoded array of notes in HomeScreen with this.props.notes:

```
export default class HomeScreen extends React.Component {
  render () {
    return (
      <View style={styles.container}>
        <NoteList navigator={this.props.navigator}
          notes={this.props.notes}/>
        ...
      </View>
    );
  }
}
```

In our ReactNotes component, we can pass the notes to the HomeScreen using props:

```
class ReactNotes extends React.Component {
  renderScene (route, navigator) {
    switch (route.name) {
      case 'home':
        return (
          <HomeScreen navigator={navigator}
          notes={[[{title:"Note 1", body:"body", id:1}, {title:"Note
2", body:"body", id:2}]]}/>
          );
      case 'createNote':
        return (
          <NoteScreen note={route.note} onChangeNote={(note) =>
console.log("note changed", note)}/>
          );
    }
  }
  ...
}
```

You may sense that we are getting tantalizingly close to our goal of being able to modify notes and see the changes in the ListView. The source of our notes is now in close proximity to the event handler that knows when the user has modified a note on the NoteScreen. What we're really talking about here is managing the state of our application.

The `ReactNotes` component is the top-level component that is responsible for managing the application state, which consists entirely of notes. So, let's make it official and move the array of notes into the component's initial state:

```
class ReactNotes extends React.Component {
  constructor(props) {
    super(props);
    this.state = {
      notes: [{title: "Note 1", body: "body", id: 1}, {title:
        "Note 2", body: "body", id: 2}]};
  }
  renderScene(route, navigator) {
    switch (route.name) {
      case 'home':
        return (
          <HomeScreen navigator={navigator}
            notes={this.state.notes}/>
        );
      case 'createNote':
        return (
          <NoteScreen note={route.note} onChangeNote={(note) =>
            console.log("note changed", note)}/>
        );
    }
  }

  . . .

}
```

Storing notes in an array makes it a little tricky to update a particular note; let's do a quick refactor using an object instead of an array, as shown:

```
class ReactNotes extends React.Component {

  constructor(props) {
    super(props);
    this.state = {
      selectedNote: {title:"", body:""},
      notes: {
        1: {title: "Note 1", body: "body", id: 1},
        2: {title: "Note 2", body: "body", id: 2}
      }
    }
  }
  ...
}
```

Now, `notes` is the object in which the keys correspond to the `ids` of the notes. Since the `NoteList` component is still expecting an array, let's use `underscore.js` to do the conversion:

```
<HomeScreen navigator={navigator} notes={_(this.state.notes).
toArray()} />
```

The `NoteList` should continue to function the way it did earlier; we are just keeping track of our notes a little differently.

Here are the changes that we need to make for the `onChangeNote` handler to actually update a note via state:

```
class ReactNotes extends React.Component {
  ...
  updateNote(note) {
    var newNotes = Object.assign({}, this.state.notes);
    newNotes[note.id] = note;
    this.setState({notes:newNotes});
  }

  renderScene(route, navigator) {
    switch (route.name) {
      case 'createNote':

        return (
          <NoteScreen note={this.state.selectedNote}
onChangeNote={(note) => this.updateNote(note)}/>
        );
    }
  }
  ...
}
```

Let's walk through the `updateNote` function to understand what's happening. First, we create a copy of `this.state.notes` using `Object.assign()`. Any time you work with nested data in your state object, we recommend making a copy like this to avoid unexpected behavior. React compares the two objects to determine if a component's state has changed and needs to be re-rendered; hence, using a copy like this ensures that the old state and the new state point to different objects. We then put our modified note into `newNotes` using `note.id` as the key. Lastly, we call `setState()` to replace the entire notes object with the new copy.

We've got a few more refactorings to do before we can try out our handiwork. Now that we know how to pass callbacks to our components via props, we can eliminate the need to pass in a navigator to the HomeScreen and NoteList components, and instead pass in a callback so that the NoteList can tell us when the user has selected a note:

```
class ReactNotes extends React.Component {
  renderScene(route, navigator) {
    switch (route.name) {
      case 'home':
        return (<HomeScreen navigator={navigator}
        notes={_(this.state.notes).toArray()}
        onSelectNote={(note) => navigator.push({name:"createNote",
        note: note})}/>);
      case 'createNote':
      return (
          <NoteScreen note={route.note} onChangeNote={(note) =>
          this.updateNote(note)}/>
        );
    }
  }
}
```

This means that we have to update our HomeScreen to pass the onSelectNote callback into the NoteList:

```
export default class HomeScreen extends React.Component {
  render () {
    return (
      <View style={styles.container}>
        <NoteList notes={this.props.notes}
          onSelectNote={this.props.onSelectNote}/>
        <Text style={styles.noNotesText}>You haven't created any
          notes!</Text>
        <SimpleButton
          onPress={() => this.props.navigator.push({
            name: 'createNote'
          })}
          customText="Create Note"
          style={styles.simpleButton}
          textStyle={styles.simpleButtonText}
        />
      </View>
    );
  }
}
```

Also, we'll have to update `NoteList`. We no longer need the `_onPress` handler or a reference to the navigator, we can just invoke the provided callback with `rowData`:

```
export default class NoteList extends React.Component {

  constructor (props) {
    super(props);
    this.ds = new ListView.DataSource({rowHasChanged: (r1, r2) => r1
!== r2});
  }
  render() {
    return (
      <ListView
        dataSource={this.ds.cloneWithRows(this.props.notes)}
        renderRow={(rowData) => {
            return (
          <TouchableHighlight
            onPress={() => this.props.onSelectNote(rowData)}
            style={styles.rowStyle}
            underlayColor="#9E7CE3"
          >
            <Text style={styles.rowText}>{rowData.title}</Text>
          </TouchableHighlight>                )
            }
        }/>
      )
  }
}

var styles = StyleSheet.create({
  rowStyle: {
    borderBottomColor: '#9E7CE3',
    borderBottomWidth: 1,
    padding: 20,
  },
  rowText: {
    fontWeight: '600'
  }
});
```

You should now be able to reload the application, touch a note, change the title, go back, and see the updated title appear in the `NoteList`, as shown in the following screenshot:

When you select a note and navigate to the `NoteScreen`, the title that appears in the `NavigationBar` is still **Create Note**. Let's modify it, so that even if we select an existing note from the list, we use the note's title instead of **Create Note**:

```
Title: function(route, navigator, index, navState) {
  switch (route.name) {
    case 'home':
      return (
        <Text style={styles.navBarTitleText}>React Notes</Text>
      );
```

```
      case 'createNote':
        return (
          <Text style={styles.navBarTitleText}>{route.note ?
            route.note.title : 'Create Note'}</Text>
        );
    }
  }
```

When you reload the application, the `NoteScreen` should reflect the title of the selected note:

Creating new notes

So far, we've been updating existing notes. How do we add new ones? Well, that's actually very easy. We just need to update the **Create Note** button in the `NavigationBar`, as shown:

```
RightButton: function(route, navigator, index, navState) {
  switch (route.name) {
    case 'home':
      return (
        <SimpleButton
          onPress={() => {
            navigator.push({
              name: 'createNote',
              note: {
                id: new Date().getTime(),
                title: '',
                body: ''
              }
            });
          }}
          customText='Create Note'
          style={styles.navBarRightButton}
          textStyle={styles.navBarButtonText}
        />
      );
    default:
      return null;
  }
}
```

As you can see, we're now passing an empty note with a generated id. (A better approach to generate ids will be to use a `uuid` generator, but we'll leave that as an exercise for the reader!)

That's it! We finally have a full, end-to-end note taking application! However, our notes only exist in memory. We need to be able to save notes to the device, so let's meet our new friend, `AsyncStorage`.

Using AsyncStorage

React Native provides an abstraction over the native local storage mechanism so that you don't have to worry about the underlying differences between how iOS and Android save data to the device.

It's really simple to use, so let's update our `ReactNotes` component to use `AsyncStorage`. First, let's add `AsyncStorage` to our list of imports:

```
import React, {
  AppRegistry,
  Navigator,
  StyleSheet,
  Text,
  AsyncStorage
} from 'react-native';
```

Next, let's add a `saveNotes()` function:

```
async saveNotes(notes) {
  try {
    await AsyncStorage.setItem("@ReactNotes:notes",
      JSON.stringify(notes));
  } catch (error) {
    console.log('AsyncStorage error: ' + error.message);
  }
}
```

You may be wondering what the `async` and `await` keywords are doing in your JavaScript! These are new keywords in ES7 that simplify working with promises. The `AsyncStorage` methods are, well, asynchronous and they return promises. Without going into too much detail, the `async` keyword in front of a function allows us to use the await keyword within the function body. The await keyword will resolve the promise, and if there's a problem, it will throw an error.

Let's modify our `updateNote` function to call our new `saveNotes` function:

```
updateNote(note) {
  var newNotes = Object.assign({}, this.state.notes);
  newNotes[note.id] = note;
  this.setState({notes:newNotes});
  this.saveNotes(newNotes);
}
```

We'll also need a function to `loadNotes` from `AsyncStorage`:

```
async loadNotes() {
  try {
    var notes = await AsyncStorage.getItem("@ReactNotes:notes");
    if (notes !== null) {
      this.setState({notes:JSON.parse(notes)})
    }
  } catch (error) {
```

```
      console.log('AsyncStorage error: ' + error.message);
    }
  }
```

We want to load our saved notes from the device in our constructor:

```
constructor(props) {
  super(props);
  this.state = {
    notes: {
      1: {title: "Note 1", body: "body", id: 1},
      2: {title: "Note 2", body: "body", id: 2}
    }
  }
  this.loadNotes();
}
```

Reload your application, and save the changes made to a note or create a new note. Then reload the application again. Your changes have been saved! We just have one more job to do, deleting notes!

Deleting notes

The last thing we need to do before we have a fully functional note-taking application is to add a **Delete** button to our `NoteScreen`. To accomplish that, we'll update our `NavigationBarRouteMapper` to add a `RightButton` when the route name is `createNote`:

```
RightButton: function(route, navigator, index, navState) {
  switch (route.name) {
    case 'home':
      return (
        <SimpleButton
          onPress={() => {
            navigator.push({
              name: 'createNote',
              note: {
                id: new Date().getTime(),
                title: '',
                body: '',
                isSaved: false
              }
            });
          }}
          customText='Create Note'
```

```
              style={styles.navBarRightButton}
              textStyle={styles.navBarButtonText}
          />
        );
      case 'createNote':
        if (route.note.isSaved) {
          return (
            <SimpleButton
              onPress={
                () => {
                  navigator.props.onDeleteNote(route.note);
                  navigator.pop();
                }
              }
              customText='Delete'
              style={styles.navBarRightButton}
              textStyle={styles.navBarButtonText}
            />
          );
        } else {
          return null;
        }
      default:
        return null;
    }
  },
```

The first thing to notice is that I've added a condition to check if the note has already been saved (we will need to tweak our updateNote function to set this). This is to make sure that the **Delete** button doesn't show up for new notes. The Create Note onPress handler has been updated to set isSaved = false in the empty note that we pass to the NoteScreen, when that button is pressed.

Now, let's look at the onPress handler for the **Delete** button:

```
            onPress={
              () => {
                navigator.props.onDeleteNote(route.note);
                navigator.pop();
              }
            }
```

We've seen `navigator.pop()` before, but we're also invoking a new callback called `onDeleteNote`. We need to pass that callback in through props in our `ReactNotes` `render` function:

```
render () {
  return (
    <Navigator
      initialRoute={{name: 'home'}}
      renderScene={this.renderScene.bind(this)}
      navigationBar={
        <Navigator.NavigationBar
          routeMapper={NavigationBarRouteMapper}
          style={styles.navBar}
        />
      }
      onDeleteNote={(note) => this.deleteNote(note)}
    />
  );
}
```

Next, we need to modify our `updateNote` function to mark the notes that have been saved:

```
updateNote(note) {
  var newNotes = Object.assign({}, this.state.notes);
  note.isSaved = true;
  newNotes[note.id] = note;
  this.setState({notes:newNotes});
  this.saveNotes(newNotes);
}
```

Just below that, we'll add the `deleteNote` function:

```
deleteNote(note) {
  var newNotes = Object.assign({}, this.state.notes);
  delete newNotes[note.id];
  this.setState({notes:newNotes});
  this.saveNotes(newNotes);
}
```

That's it! Reload the application and create a new note. Notice that there is no **Delete** button in the NavigationBar. Press the **Back** button to view the note in the list, then tap that item in the list to view it. You should be able to see the **Delete** button in the top right corner, as shown:

Press the **Delete** button and you will be returned to the HomeScreen where the deleted note will disappear from the list!

Summary

In this chapter, we have created a complete note-taking application. You have learned how to use the `ListView` to display data, pass data into components using props, keep track of a component's state, and save data to the device using AsyncStorage. Moreover, you have done did all of this without writing any `platform-specific` code!

6
Working with Geolocation and Maps

So far you've seen that React Native simplifies the creation of native UI components, such as lists, text fields, and buttons, and it gives you simple abstractions, such as AsyncStorage, to work with underlying native APIs. Soon, you'll see that you also have access to advanced components, such as maps using the `MapView` component, and that you can access more advanced native features, such as geolocation using React Native's Geolocation API. We'll demonstrate these capabilities by adding the ability to capture and save current GPS coordinates with each new note. Note that the next two chapters will focus on iOS development, as the feature set for Android is not complete.

In this chapter we will cover the following topics:

- Learning how to get the current geolocation
- Listening for changes to the user's position
- Ensuring that our app requires appropriate permissions
- Saving location data with each note
- Displaying the original locations of all the notes on a `MapView`

Let's get started!

Introducing the Geolocation API

React Native provides an easy-to-use abstraction over the native Geolocation APIs. It follows the **MDN (Mozilla Developer Network)** specification, which recommends the following geolocation interface:

```
navigator.geolocation.getCurrentPosition(success, error, options)
```

This method `asynchronously` asks for the device's current location and will call the `success` callback with a `Position` object if it is successful and the `error` callback if it fails (usually, due to misconfigured permissions in your app or the user explicitly rejecting the request to allow your app to know their location). The `options` argument allows you to request higher position accuracy, define how long you're willing to wait for a response, and specify the maximum age of cached data that you're willing to accept:

```
navigator.geolocation.watchPosition(success, error, options)
```

This function enables you to register a function that will be called each time the position changes. This function returns an integer that represents the `ID` of the callback you registered. This allows you to stop listening for updates by calling the following:

```
navigator.geolocation.clearWatch(id);
```

The location permission in iOS

Before we begin integrating geolocation into our notes, we need to configure a permission to request the user's location. From Xcode, open `info.plist` and make sure that the `NSLocationWhenInUseUsageDescription` key is located in the file (it should be enabled by default):

Once the application starts up, you should see a permission modal automatically pop up in the center of the screen:

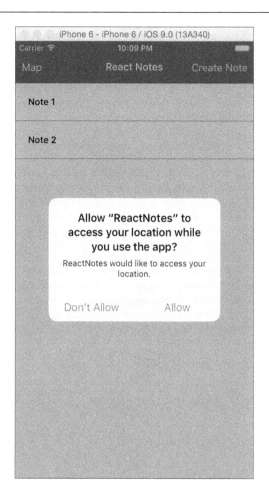

Tagging notes with geolocation

Let's take geolocation for a spin and start capturing the user's location when they save a new note. Since we're going to be using the location data when we save notes, we'll add our code to the ReactNotes component in index.ios.js or index.android.js. Let's begin by adding a function called trackLocation():

```
class ReactNotes extends React.Component {
  trackLocation() {
    navigator.geolocation.getCurrentPosition(
      (initialPosition) => this.setState({initialPosition}),
      (error) => alert(error.message)
    );
```

```
        this.watchID =
          navigator.geolocation.watchPosition((lastPosition) => {
          this.setState({lastPosition});
        });
    }


    ...
    }
```

Here we call `getCurrentPosition` and provide a callback that will update the current state with the position information returned from the device. We also provide an error handler if something goes wrong.

Next, we use `watchPosition()` to register an event handler that will be called when the user's position changes. We also save the `watchId` that is returned from this call, so that we can stop listening when the component has been unmounted. It is generally good practice to clear up any listeners you initially set up in your constructor or `componentDidMount` method from the `componentWillUnmount` function:

```
    class ReactNotes extends React.Component {
      componentWillUnmount() {
        navigator.geolocation.clearWatch(this.watchID);
      }
      trackLocation() {

        ...
      }
    ...
    }
```

Then, we'll call our `trackLocation()` function from the constructor and add some notes with the position data to our initial state:

```
    class ReactNotes extends React.Component {
      constructor (props) {
        super(props);
        StatusBarIOS.setStyle('light-content');

        this.state = {
          notes: {
            1: {
              title: "Note 1",
              body: "body",
              id: 1,
              location: {
                coords: {
```

```
                  latitude: 33.987,
                  longitude: -118.47
                }
              }
          },
          2: {
            title: "Note 2",
            body: "body",
            id: 2,
            location: {
              coords: {
                latitude: 33.986,
                longitude: -118.46
              }
            }
          }
        }
      };

      this.loadNotes();
      this.trackLocation();
    }
```

Saving the position data with a note requires a minor adjustment to our
`updateNote()` function:

```
    updateNote(note) {
      var newNotes = Object.assign({}, this.state.notes);

      if (!note.isSaved) {
        note.location = this.state.lastPosition;
      }

      note.isSaved = true;
      newNotes[note.id] = note;
      this.setState({notes:newNotes});
      this.saveNotes(newNotes);
    }
```

That's all there is to it! Reload the app, create a new note, and the GPS coordinates
will be stored when the note is saved for the first time. But how can we visualize the
position data associated with each of our notes? Let's make a `MapView` to display pins
for each note!

The complete documentation of geolocation can be found in the React Native documentation at `https://facebook.github.io/react-native/docs/geolocation.html`.

NoteLocationScreen

Now, since we are capturing the location of the user on note creation, we want to display this information in a useful manner. Location data perfectly matches up with showing the notes on a map UI. This way the user can visually see all of the notes that they have created. We are going to create a new component called `NoteLocationScreen` to house our note locations, but before writing the code for this screen, let's begin by adding the navigation.

On the home screen, we want to have a **Map** button in the `navbar` to transition to the `NoteLocationScreen`. Update the `LeftButton` and `Title` in `NavigationBarRouteMapper` to the following:

```
var NavigationBarRouteMapper = {
  LeftButton: function(route, navigator, index, navState) {
    switch (route.name) {
      case 'home':
        return (
          <SimpleButton
            onPress={() => navigator.push({name:
              'noteLocations'})}
            customText='Map'
            style={styles.navBarLeftButton}
            textStyle={styles.navBarButtonText}
          />
        );
      case 'createNote':
      case 'noteLocations':
        return (
          <SimpleButton
            onPress={() => navigator.pop()}
            customText='Back'
            style={styles.navBarLeftButton}
            textStyle={styles.navBarButtonText}
          />
        );
      default:
        return null;
    }
  },
```

```
. . .

    Title: function(route, navigator, index, navState) {
      switch (route.name) {
        case 'home':
          return (
            <Text style={styles.navBarTitleText}>React Notes</Text>
          );
        case 'createNote':
          return (
            <Text style={styles.navBarTitleText}>{route.note ?
              route.note.title : 'Create Note'}</Text>
          );
        case 'noteLocations':
          return (
            <Text style={styles.navBarTitleText}>Note
              Locations</Text>
          );
      }
    }
  }
```

Here, we are defining a new route called `noteLocations`. Notice that we also want the `back` button to be displayed on the `noteLocation` route, so we include the case along with the `createNote` route.

If you haven't already, add a new `NoteLocationScreen.js` file to `App/Components/` and import it into `ReactNotes`. The last thing we need to do is include it in our `renderScene` function. We are going to pass it in the list of notes and the same `onSelectNote` function to our `NoteLocationScreen`:

```
import NoteLocationScreen from './App/Components/NoteLocationScreen';

. . .

class ReactNotes extends React.Component {
  . . .

  renderScene(route, navigator) {
    switch (route.name) {
      case 'home':
        return (
          <HomeScreen navigator={navigator} notes={_(this.
state.notes).toArray()} onSelectNote={(note) => navigator.
push({name:"createNote", note: note})} />
```

```
        );
      case 'createNote':
        return (
          <NoteScreen note={route.note} onChangeNote={(note) => this.
updateNote(note)} />
        );
      case 'noteLocations':
        return (
          <NoteLocationScreen notes={this.state.notes}
onSelectNote={(note) => navigator.push({name:"createNote", note:
note})} />
        );
    }
  }

  ...

}
```

MapView

MapView is another component provided by React Native to display the map corresponding to each platform: Apple Maps on iOS and Google Maps on Android. You can start by adding the `MapView` to the `NoteLocationScreen`:

```
import React, {
  MapView,
  StyleSheet
} from 'react-native';

export default class NoteLocationScreen extends React.Component {
  render () {
    return (
      <MapView
        showsUserLocation={true}
        style={styles.map}
      />
    );
  }
}

var styles = StyleSheet.create({
  map: {
    flex: 1,
```

```
    marginTop: 64
  }
});
```

 If the map does not show your location on iOS, you may need to enable locations in the simulator. Set a custom location by navigating to **Debug** | **Location** | **Custom Location**.

The showsUserLocation function will zoom and display the location of the user on the map; by default, this value is false. Next, we want to gather all the notes locations to display them on our map using annotations. The annotation format accepts an object with longitude, latitude, some title information, and on press attributes. We will loop through the list of notes passed via props and extract the location data. The list of annotations is then passed to the MapView's annotations prop:

```
export default class NoteLocationScreen extends React.Component {
  render () {
    var locations = _.values(this.props.notes).map((note) => {
      return {
        latitude: note.location.coords.latitude,
        longitude: note.location.coords.longitude,
        title: note.title
      };
    });

    return (
      <MapView
        annotations={locations}
        showsUserLocation={true}
        style={styles.map}
      />
    );
  }
}
```

We can also add the ability to view the note by adding a `callout on press` function to the annotations. The `callout on press` method will invoke the `onNoteSelect` function we passed in and transition to the `NoteScreen`. Here we are adding a `left callout`:

```
export default class NoteLocationScreen extends React.Component {
  render () {
    var locations = _.values(this.props.notes).map((note) => {
      return {
        latitude: note.location.coords.latitude,
        longitude: note.location.coords.longitude,
        hasLeftCallout: true,
        onLeftCalloutPress: this.props.onSelectNote.bind(this,
          note),
```

```
            title: note.title
        };
    });

    . . .

}
```

Check the React Native documentation for more details on `MapView` at
`https://facebook.github.io/react-native/docs/mapview.html`.

Summary

In this chapter, we explored more of React Native's built-in components and modules to capture the device-specific location data. The Geolocation API provides us the mechanism which hooks into the existing component life cycle to track user location. By incorporating this into our existing saved data, we can use the longitude and latitude values to display a map of where all of our notes were taken.

7
Integrating Native Modules

So far you've seen that React Native contains a large amount of functionality right out of the box. It provides an easy way for you to use a wide variety of native features via JavaScript, but sometimes you may need something that isn't yet covered by the built-in React Native components. Luckily, React Native is fully extensible via Native Modules. Thanks to a very active community, there is a growing list of custom components that are filling in the gaps. In this chapter, we'll use one of those third-party Native Modules to add camera support to our React Notes application.

In this chapter, we'll cover the following topics:

- Installing the custom React Native camera module using npm
- Adding a CameraScreen and camera component
- Saving captured images to disk
- Displaying the captured images in the NoteImageScreen

Adding images to notes

Our note-taking application is shaping up nicely, but a picture is worth a thousand words, so wouldn't it be nice if we could take a photo and store it with a note? Since React Native does not ship with a camera component, we'll need to use a very popular component created by *Lochlan Wansbrough*. The source code can be found at: https://github.com/lwansbrough/react-native-camera.

At this point, you are most likely familiar with the addition of new screens to our navigation. Let's quickly write the navigation code for the `CameraScreen` before we include the Native Module. In the `NavigationBarRouteMapper`, add the `camera` route to the `LeftButton` and `Title` attributes:

```
var NavigationBarRouteMapper = {
  LeftButton: function(route, navigator, index, navState) {
    switch (route.name) {
      case 'home':
        return (
          <SimpleButton
            onPress={() => navigator.push({name:
              'noteLocations'})}
            customText='Map'
            style={styles.navBarLeftButton}
            textStyle={styles.navBarButtonText}
          />
        );
      case 'createNote':
      case 'noteLocations':
      case 'camera':
        return (
          <SimpleButton
            onPress={() => navigator.pop()}
            customText='Back'
            style={styles.navBarLeftButton}
            textStyle={styles.navBarButtonText}
          />
        );
      default:
        return null;
    }
  },

  ...

  Title: function(route, navigator, index, navState) {
    switch (route.name) {
      case 'home':
        return (
          <Text style={styles.navBarTitleText}>React Notes</Text>
        );
      case 'createNote':
        return (
```

```
          <Text style={styles.navBarTitleText}>{route.note ?
            route.note.title : 'Create Note'}</Text>
        );
      case 'noteLocations':
        return (
          <Text style={styles.navBarTitleText}>
            Note Locations</Text>
        );
      case 'camera':
        return (
          <Text style={styles.navBarTitleText}>Take Picture</Text>
        );
      }
    }
  };
```

Then, in the `ReactNotes` component update the `renderScene` method:

```
class ReactNotes extends React.Component {
  ...

  renderScene(route, navigator) {
    switch (route.name) {
      ...

      case 'createNote':
        return (
          <NoteScreen navigator={navigator} note={route.note}
onChangeNote={(note) => this.updateNote(note)} showCameraButton={true}
/>
        );

      case 'camera':
        return (
          <CameraScreen />
        );
      }
    }

  ...

}
```

We pass in another prop called `showCameraButton` to the `NoteScreen`, which we will use later to hide the camera button from the android version.

> The same `showCameraButton` prop, except of value `false`, should be passed from the `renderScene` method for the Android version of ReactNotes: `showCameraButton={false}`.

Installing react-native-camera on iOS

There are three steps to install react-native-camera and to include it in our `CameraScreen`. From the command line, navigate to the `ReactNotes` directory and run the following command:

```
npm install react-native-camera@0.3.8 --save
```

If you take a look at the `node_modules` directory in the `ReactNotes` project you'll see a new directory named `react-native-camera`, which contains both the JavaScript and native source code of the module. In the `ios` subdirectory, you'll notice a file called `RCTCamera.xcodeproj`, as shown in the following screenshot:

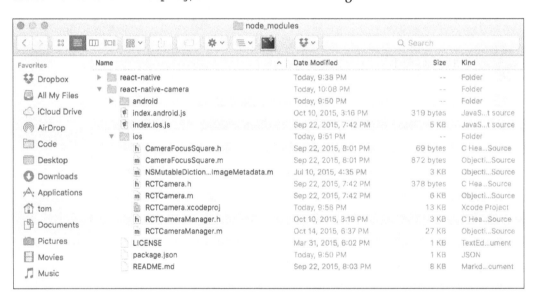

We need to add this file to our Xcode project's library. In the Xcode project navigator, right-click on **Libraries** and choose **Add Files to ReactNotes**:

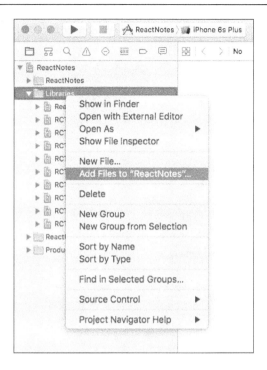

In the Finder window that appears, navigate to **ReactNotes | node_modules | react-native-camera | ios**, select **RCTCamera.xcodeproj** and click **Add**:

Take a look at the **Libraries** folder in the project navigator and you should see **RCTCamera.xcodeproj** in the list.

Next, select **ReactNotes** in the project navigator, click on **Build Phases** and expand the **Link Binary With Libraries** section:

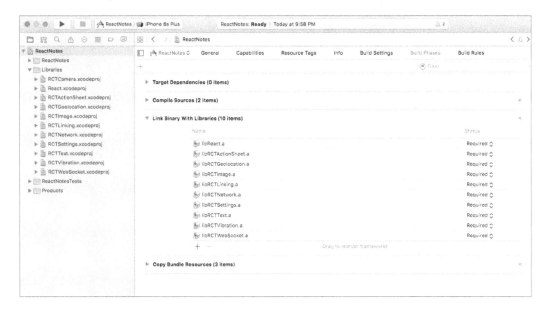

Click the plus sign at the bottom of the **Link Binary with Libraries section**, select **libRCTCamera.a** from the list and click **Add**:

We're now ready to use the camera component in our application.

Searching for Native Modules

A brief note before we start using the camera component is how you can find these modules on your own. The two best places to look for open source Native Modules are either on GitHub (`https://github.com`) or NPM (`https://www.npmjs.com`). A search on either of these sites will give you plenty of third-party modules created by the React Native community to use in your projects.

Using the camera component

The hard part is over! Importing the camera module is as simple as including any other React component:

```
import Camera from 'react-native-camera';
```

Using the Camera component is quite simple, as well. Here's the `render` function of the `CameraScreen`:

```
render () {
  return (
    <Camera
      captureTarget={Camera.constants.CaptureTarget.disk}
      ref="cam"
      style={styles.container}
    >
      <View style={styles.cameraButtonContainer}>
        <SimpleButton
          onPress={this._takePicture.bind(this)}
          customText="Capture"
          style={styles.cameraButton}
          textStyle={styles.cameraButtonText}
        />
      </View>
    </Camera>
  );
}
```

The Camera module exposes a number of props that you can use to customize its behavior but most of the default values work well for our purpose. However, you'll note that we set the `captureTarget` property to `Camera.constants.CaptureTarget.disk`. This setting will place the saved images into a directory on the device that only our `ReactNotes` application has access to. The default value for the `captureTarget` property is `Camera.constants.CaptureTarget.cameraRoll`, which will put the image in the shared location used by the native camera when you're taking pictures. Although that will normally be acceptable, at the time of this writing there is a bug that prevents ReactNative from loading images from that location.

Take a look at the code listing above. Notice that we've added child components to the camera component. It behaves just like a `View` component; you're now familiar with laying out children using the `Flexbox` attribute. In our example, we've added a `View` and a `SimpleButton` with an `onPress` handler that will capture the image:

```
_takePicture () {
  this.refs.cam.capture((err, data) => {
    if (err) return;
    this.props.onPicture(data);
  });
}
```

Recall that we added `ref="cam"` to the camera component declaration; thus, allowing us to refer to it in our handler. When we call the `capture()` function, we pass in a callback that takes two arguments, `err` (which should be null unless the user doesn't permit `ReactNotes` to use the camera) and data, which will include the full path to the image once it is saved to disk.

In order to save the path to the image along with the note, we'll need to pass the data up using `this.props.onPicture(data)`. We'll need to update our top-level `ReactNotes` component, but before we do that, here's the complete code for the `CameraScreen`:

```
import React, {
  StyleSheet,
  Text,
  View
} from 'react-native';

import Camera from 'react-native-camera';
import SimpleButton from './SimpleButton';

export default class CameraScreen extends React.Component {
  _takePicture () {
```

```
      this.refs.cam.capture((err, data) => {
        if (err) return;
        this.props.onPicture(data);
      });
    }

    render () {
      return (
        <Camera
          captureTarget={Camera.constants.CaptureTarget.disk}
          ref="cam"
          style={styles.container}
        >
          <View style={styles.cameraButtonContainer}>
            <SimpleButton
              onPress={this._takePicture.bind(this)}
              customText="Capture"
              style={styles.cameraButton}
              textStyle={styles.cameraButtonText}
            />
          </View>
        </Camera>
      );
    }
  }

  var styles = StyleSheet.create({
    container: {
      flex: 1,
      marginTop: 64
    },
    cameraButtonContainer: {
      position: 'absolute',
      bottom: 20,
      left: 20,
      right: 20
    },
    cameraButton: {
      backgroundColor: '#5B29C1',
      borderRadius: 4,
      paddingHorizontal: 20,
      paddingVertical: 15
    },
```

```
      cameraButtonText: {
        color: 'white',
        textAlign: 'center'
      }
    });
```

Return to `index.ios.js` and add the `onPicture` callback to the `CameraScreen` props:

```
    renderScene(route, navigator) {
        switch (route.name) {
          case 'home':
            return (

            ...

          case 'camera':
            return (
                <CameraScreen onPicture={(imagePath) => this.
    saveNoteImage(imagePath, route.note)}/>
            );

        ...

        }
      }
    }
```

We're passing in a callback that takes an `imagePath` and then calls `this.saveNoteImage(imagePath, route.note)`. Let's add that function just above `renderScene`:

```
    saveNoteImage(imagePath, note) {
      note.imagePath = imagePath;
      this.updateNote(note);
    }
```

This function simply takes the `imagePath`, adds it to the note object, and passes the modified note to our `updateNote()` function.

Now you can run the application in the simulator, click the **Take Picture** button and the screen becomes black! Don't worry, there's nothing wrong with your code; the iOS simulator doesn't have access to a camera, so it displays a black screen. However, if you click the **Capture** button, an image will be saved to your file system and when you return to view the image you'll actually see a white screen.

To verify if this works, you can `console.log` the `imagePath`, navigate to the image, modify the image, and then return to the `NoteImageScreen` to see your changes.

Viewing images

With images, it is important that they are getting saved to the `imagePath` attribute correctly, we want to be able to view them again. We will add another screen called `NoteImageScreen` that displays the image captured by the camera component. In the `App/Components/` directory, create the `NoteImageScreen.js` file. Same as before, we are going to include this in the navigation as shown:

```
import NoteImageScreen from './App/Components/NoteImageScreen';

var NavigationBarRouteMapper = {
  LeftButton: function(route, navigator, index, navState) {
    switch (route.name) {

      ...

      case 'createNote':
      case 'noteLocations':
      case 'camera':
      case 'noteImage':
        ...
    }
  },

  ...

  Title: function(route, navigator, index, navState) {
    switch (route.name) {

      ...

      case 'noteImage':
        return (
          <Text style={styles.navBarTitleText}>{`Image: ${route.note.
title}`}</Text>
        );
    }
  }
};

class ReactNotes extends React.Component {

  ...
```

```
renderScene(route, navigator) {
  switch (route.name) {

    . . .

    case 'noteImage':
      return (
        <NoteImageScreen note={route.note} />
      );
  }
}

. . .

}
```

You might notice that in the title code for the `noteImage` route we use another ES6 feature known as string interpolation. This allows us to format a string directly between the back ticks `` `${variable}` `` with the value of a variable, in this case its `route.note.title`.

The image component

The Image component is provided by React Native to display images from various sources, such as the local disk or over a network. To render our image, all we have to do is pass in the `imagePath` from our note to the source prop. In the `ImageNoteScreen` add:

```
import React, {
  Image,
  View,
  StyleSheet
} from 'react-native';

export default class NoteImageScreen extends React.Component {
  render () {
    return (
      <View style={styles.container}>
        <Image
          source={{uri: this.props.note.imagePath}}
          style={styles.image}
        />
      </View>
    );
```

```
    }
  }

  var styles = StyleSheet.create({
    container: {
      flex: 1,
      marginTop: 64
    },
    image: {
      flex: 1
    }
  });
```

Here, we specify an object with an `uri` attribute to pass in the path. You can also use a `url` from the internet to render images this way also:

```
  source={{uri: https://example.com/example.png}}
```

To require images locally just specify the path to the image:

```
  source={require('./example.png')}
```

For more information on the Image component, see the React Native documentation at `https://facebook.github.io/react-native/docs/image.html`.

Deleting images

In case the user takes the wrong picture, we need a way to be able to remove the image from a note. Similar to the navigation of the `NoteScreen`, we are going to add a `delete` button to the right-hand side. In the `ReactNotes` component, we are going to add the `deleteNoteImage` method to remove the `imagePath` attribute from the note:

```
  class ReactNotes extends React.Component {

    ...

    deleteNoteImage (note) {
      note.imagePath = null;
      this.updateNote(note);
    }

    saveNoteImage(imagePath, note) {
      note.imagePath = imagePath;
```

```
        this.updateNote(note);
    }

    ...

}
```

This looks similar to our `saveNoteImage` function, except that we are setting the value to `null`. Next, to add the button, we once again add the `noteImage` attribute to the `RightButton` function in `NavigationBarRouteMapper` and pass the `deleteNoteImage` function to the Navigator component:

```
var NavigationBarRouteMapper = {

    ...

    RightButton: function(route, navigator, index, navState) {
        switch (route.name) {

            ...

            case 'noteImage':
                return (
                    <SimpleButton
                        onPress={() => {
                            navigator.props.onDeleteNoteImage(route.note);
                            navigator.pop();
                        }}
                        customText='Delete'
                        style={styles.navBarRightButton}
                        textStyle={styles.navBarButtonText}
                    />
                );
            default:
                return null;
        }
    },

    ...

}

class ReactNotes extends React.Component {

    ...
```

```
render () {
  return (
    <Navigator
      initialRoute={{name: 'home'}}
      renderScene={this.renderScene.bind(this)}
      navigationBar={
        <Navigator.NavigationBar
          routeMapper={NavigationBarRouteMapper}
          style={styles.navBar}
        />
      }
      onDeleteNote={(note) => this.deleteNote(note)}
      onDeleteNoteImage={(note) => this.deleteNoteImage(note)}
    />
  );
}
}
```

Connecting the final pieces

Now that we have `CameraScreen` and `ImageScreen`, we need to be able to navigate to them via the `NoteScreen`. We are going to add a button that will change the state based on the `imagePath` of the note. If it does not exist, then we want the user to transition to the `CameraScreen` and the `ImageScreen` when it does. Visually we are going to place the button in-line with the title input:

```
import SimpleButton = from './SimpleButton';

export default class NoteScreen extends React.Component {

  ...

  blurInputs () {
    this.refs.body.blur();
    this.refs.title.blur();
  }

  render () {
    var pictureButton = null;
    if (this.props.showCameraButton) {
      pictureButton = (this.state.note.imagePath) ? (
        <SimpleButton
          onPress={() => {
            this.blurInputs();
```

```
              this.props.navigator.push({
                name: 'noteImage',
                note: this.state.note
              });
          }}
          customText="View Picture"
          style={styles.takePictureButton}
          textStyle={styles.takePictureButtonText}
        />
      ) : (
        <SimpleButton
          onPress={() => {
            this.blurInputs();
            this.props.navigator.push({
              name: 'camera',
              note: this.state.note
            });
          }}
          customText="Take Picture"
          style={styles.takePictureButton}
          textStyle={styles.takePictureButtonText}
        />
      );
  }

  return (
    <View style={styles.container}>
      <View style={styles.inputContainer}>
        <TextInput
          ref="title"
          autoFocus={true}
          autoCapitalize="sentences"
          placeholder="Untitled"
          style={[styles.textInput, styles.title]}
          onEndEditing={(text) => {this.refs.body.focus()}}
          underlineColorAndroid="transparent"
          value={this.state.note.title}
          onChangeText={(title) => this.updateNote(title, this.
state.note.body)}
        />

        {pictureButton}
```

```
        </View>
            . . .

        </View>
    );
    }
}
```

Note that if the `showCameraButton` prop is enabled, we render a different button to
indicate the next step to the user based on the existence of the `imagePath`. Each of the
corresponding functions on the `SimpleButtons` will push the camera or `noteImage`
route onto the navigator stack.

 `blurInputs` is a function that we defined to disable the focus on
the `TextInputs` and to hide the keyboard when transitioning to
the next screen.

The styles for the button are similar to what we have had before. The main difference
is the padding around the text:

```
var styles = StyleSheet.create({

    . . .

    takePictureButton: {
        backgroundColor: '#5B29C1',
        borderColor: '#48209A',
        borderWidth: 1,
        borderRadius: 4,
        paddingHorizontal: 10,
        paddingVertical: 5,
        shadowColor: 'darkgrey',
        shadowOffset: {
            width: 1,
            height: 1
        },
        shadowOpacity: 0.8,
        shadowRadius: 1
    },
    takePictureButtonText: {
        color: 'white'
    }
});
```

We can place the button in the same line as the `TextInput` since the `inputContainer` style we defined earlier has a `flexDirection` of row, as shown:

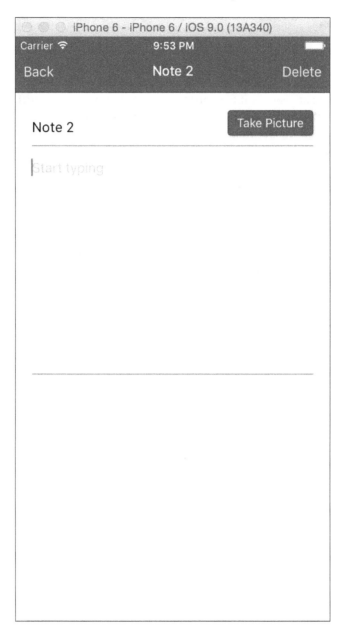

Summary

In this chapter, you learned that even if React Native lacks a feature you need, you'll be able to find a Native Module that suits your needs. In our case, we need camera support for our note taking the application and we showed you how to install a great third-party module via npm. We created a new screen for our Camera component and wired it up to our note saving mechanism to store the path of the image that is captured. We then created a NoteImage screen to view the captured image and added a way to delete the images we captured.

Facebook exposes native device functionality in exactly the same way that react-native-camera does. If you're curious, you can take a look at the very simple vibration module that ships with React Native: https://github.com/facebook/react-native/tree/master/Libraries/Vibration. Even if you do not consider yourself an Objective-C, Swift, or Java programmer, don't be afraid to try creating a Native Module yourself—you might be surprised by how easy it is!

8
Releasing the Application

The first version of our application is complete, which means that we are ready to go through the process of creating the production builds. In this chapter, we will start by showing you how to generate and run the application off of a static JavaScript bundle. Then, in preparation for the App Store, we will use Xcode to build our iOS release. Lastly, for Android we will walk through the set of command-line tools and scripts provided by React Native to build the final APK.

In this chapter, we will cover the following:

- Generating the static bundle for iOS
- Using the `static bundle` in place of `react-native start`
- Building a release in Xcode
- Signing and building the Android release APK

Generating the static bundle in iOS

So far, we have been serving the application's static bundle (where all of our JavaScript code lives) from a node server started by either Xcode or a terminal using `react-native start`. Before we create releases for iOS and Android, we need to generate the static JS bundle that our application will load. We will begin by creating the release in iOS; for Android, skip to the `generating the Android APK` section.

Once again, we are going to use the `react-native-cli` and execute the `bundle` command. The `bundle` command requires three flags: `c`, `platform`, and `bundle-output`. The `entry-file` specifies the path to the root component, the platform is either iOS or Android, and `bundle-output` is the path to place the generated bundle.

From the terminal in the root directory, run `react-native bundle` with an `entry-file` of `index.ios.js`, platform `iOS`, and point the path of the `bundle-output` to `ios/main.jsbundle`:

```
$ react-native bundle --entry-file index.ios.js --platform ios
--bundle-output ios/main.jsbundle
bundle: Created ReactPackager
bundle: Closing client
bundle: start
bundle: finish
bundle: Writing bundle output to: ios/main.jsbundle
bundle: Done writing bundle output
```

Assets destination folder is not set, skipping...

More details about `react-native bundle` for iOS can be found in the React Native documentation at `https://facebook.github.io/react-native/docs/running-on-device-ios.html#using-offline-bundle`.

Testing the static bundle in iOS

First, we need to test that the static bundle can be loaded by our iOS application in the simulator. Open `AppDelegate.m` in Xcode and take a look at the following code and comments:

```
 * Loading JavaScript code - uncomment the one you want.
 *
 * OPTION 1
 * Load from development server. Start the server from the
repository root:
 *
 * $ npm start
 *
 * To run on device, change `localhost` to the IP address of your
computer
 * (you can get this by typing `ifconfig` into the terminal and
selecting the
 * `inet` value under `en0:`) and make sure your computer and iOS
device are
 * on the same Wi-Fi network.
 */

  jsCodeLocation = [NSURL URLWithString:@"http://localhost:8081/index.
ios.bundle?platform=ios&dev=true"];

/**
 * OPTION 2
```

```
    * Load from pre-bundled file on disk. To re-generate the static
bundle
    * from the root of your project directory, run
    *
    * $ react-native bundle --minify
    *
    * see http://facebook.github.io/react-native/docs/runningondevice.
html
    */

//    jsCodeLocation = [[NSBundle mainBundle] URLForResource:@"main"
withExtension:@"jsbundle"];
```

The various methods of loading the JavaScript bundle are outlined here. We are interested in OPTION 2, loading a pre-bundled file from the disk. Comment out the jsCodeLocation statement from OPTION 1 and uncomment the second in OPTION 2:

```
// jsCodeLocation = [NSURL URLWithString:@"http://localhost:8081/
index.ios.bundle?platform=ios&dev=true"];
...

jsCodeLocation = [[NSBundle mainBundle] URLForResource:@"main"
withExtension:@"jsbundle"];
```

Make sure that no react-native start terminal sessions are running, then build and run the application from Xcode (*Cmd + R*). You should be at the top of the simulator to indicate that it is loading from a pre-bundled file:

Creating an iOS release in Xcode

In order to submit to the AppStore, we need to build our application for distribution. Luckily, the Xcode project we initially created with `react-native init` has some of this preconfigured for us. First, we want to change our **Build Configuration** to **disable** features, such as the developer menu that we get while we are debugging.

Let's configure the iOS release:

1. In Xcode, navigate to **Product | Scheme | Edit Scheme...** and select **Run**, and under the **Info** tab change **Build Configuration** from **Debug** to **Release**:

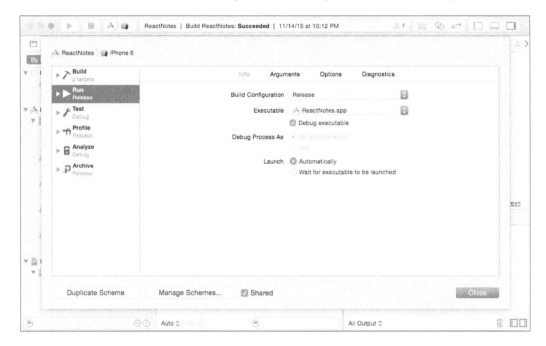

2. Target the **iOS Device** instead of the simulator:

3. Finally, run the build from **Product | Archive**. The **Organizer** window will open a list of archives for your project. You can return to this screen later by selecting **Window | Organizer** from the top menu:

4. In the future, when you create multiple releases, you should increase the version number found in **Targets | ReactNotes | General**. For the purposes of our first release, this can be disregarded:

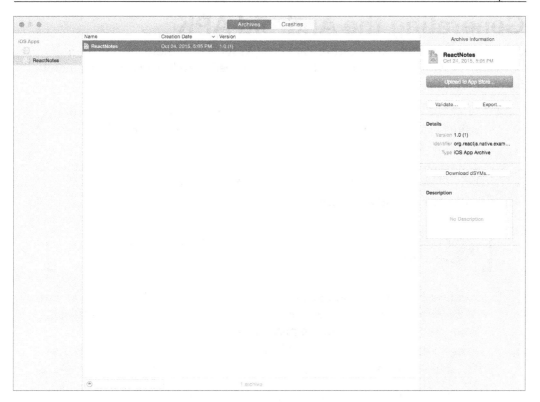

Once your build has been archived, it is ready to be submitted to the Apple App Store. This book doesn't cover the application to the App Store but the next steps will be available on the Apple developer website at https://developer.apple.com.

Generating the Android APK

Building the **Android Application Package** (**APK**) is a bit more cryptic than releasing for iOS. There are a few steps that we need to follow before we generate the static bundle, like we did in iOS:

1. First, we need to generate a key that we can use to sign our application using `keytool`. Navigate to the `android/app` folder in a terminal and run this command:

```
$ keytool -genkey -v -keystore my-release-key.keystore -alias my-
key-alias -keyalg RSA -keysize 2048 -validity 10000

[Storing my-release-key.keystore]
```

 Note that this is a private file and should never be shared with anyone. Keep it somewhere safe!

2. Next we have a few configuration files to update. Up a level in the `android/` directory open `gradle.properties` and add these four lines, replacing YOUR_KEY_PASSWORD with the password you used for `keytool`:

```
MYAPP_RELEASE_STORE_FILE=my-release-key.keystore MYAPP_RELEASE_
KEY_ALIAS=my-key-alias MYAPP_RELEASE_STORE_PASSWORD=YOUR_KEY_
PASSWORD
MYAPP_RELEASE_KEY_PASSWORD= YOUR_KEY_PASSWORD
```

3. Add the following in `android/app/build.gradle`:

```
android {
    ...

    signingConfigs {
        release {
            storeFile file(MYAPP_RELEASE_STORE_FILE)
            storePassword MYAPP_RELEASE_STORE_PASSWORD
            keyAlias MYAPP_RELEASE_KEY_ALIAS
            keyPassword MYAPP_RELEASE_KEY_PASSWORD
        }
    }
    buildTypes {
        release {
            ...
            signingConfig signingConfigs.release
        }
    }
}
```

4. Now, we can generate the static bundle for Android. Create a new directory `android/app/src/main/assets/` and run this modified form of the `react-native bundle` command:

```
react-native bundle --platform android --dev false --entry-file
index.android.js --bundle-output android/app/src/main/assets/
index.android.bundle --assets-dest android/app/src/main/res/
```

This gives the following output:

```
$ react-native bundle --platform android --dev false --entry-file
index.android.js --bundle-output android/app/src/main/assets/
index.android.bundle --assets-dest android/app/src/main/res/

Building package...

transforming [=======================================] 100%
326/326

Build complete

Successfully saved bundle to android/app/src/main/assets/index.
android.bundle
```

5. Build the final APK in the `android/ directory` using the `gradle` command:

```
./gradlew assembleRelease
```

If you have set up the key signing correctly, you can test your release in the simulator or on a device with the following:

```
./gradlew installRelease
```

6. With this, we have our final release APK (that can be found in `android/app/build/outputs/apk/app-release.apk`). Check out the launch checklist on Android developers for more information on the Play Store submission process at `https://developer.android.com/distribute/tools/launch-checklist.html`.

Summary

In this chapter, you learned how to build a release of our application in preparation for submitting it to the App Store or Google Play Store. iOS had a pre-configuration scheme in Xcode to disable the developer features. We then created an archive by targeting the iOS device. On Android, we created a private release key with **keytool** and built the release APK using the command line and `gradle`. It is important to follow up and test that both of these release builds work before submission, to decrease the likelihood of rejection.

We hope that this book gave you the fundamentals you need to start creating mobile apps with React Native. Although React and React Native are still very early in terms of development, you can expect the core concepts discussed in this book to stay relevant for some time to come. When Android finally reaches feature parity with iOS, the doors will open for a lot more rapid development between the two platforms. Good luck, and we can't wait to see your apps out there on the App and Google Play Stores!

Index

A

Android Application Package (APK)
  generating 144, 145
Android Material Theme
  changing 66, 67
  reference 67
Apple Developer
  URL 143
application
  running, on Android emulator 25, 26
  structuring 28
AsyncStorage
  using 95-97

C

components
  about 15
  creating 15, 16
  JavaScript XML (JSX) 16
  props 18
  state 19, 20
  Text component 17
  View component 17
CSS-layout repository
  reference 54

F

Flexbox
  about 54
  flex container 54-56

flex container
  about 54-56
  absolute positioning 62
  flex items 56, 57
  horizontal centering 57-62
  vertical centering 57-62
flexDirection property
  about 54
  column 54
  rows 54

G

geolocation API
  about 104
  location permission, in iOS 104
  notes, tagging with 105-107
  reference, for documentation 108
GitHub
  URL 123

I

Image component 128, 129
images
  deleting 129
  viewing 127, 128
iOS release
  creating, in Xcode 140-143
iOS Simulator
  starter template, running in 24, 25

V

View component 17
Virtual DOM 13, 14

X

Xcode
  command-line tools (CLT) 2
  for running starter template, in iOS
     simulator 24, 25
  installing 2
  iOS release, creating in 140-143
  sample application,
     experimenting with 10, 11
  sample application, preview 6-9
  sample application, running 3-5

Thank you for buying
Getting Started with React Native

About Packt Publishing

Packt, pronounced 'packed', published its first book, *Mastering phpMyAdmin for Effective MySQL Management*, in April 2004, and subsequently continued to specialize in publishing highly focused books on specific technologies and solutions.

Our books and publications share the experiences of your fellow IT professionals in adapting and customizing today's systems, applications, and frameworks. Our solution-based books give you the knowledge and power to customize the software and technologies you're using to get the job done. Packt books are more specific and less general than the IT books you have seen in the past. Our unique business model allows us to bring you more focused information, giving you more of what you need to know, and less of what you don't.

Packt is a modern yet unique publishing company that focuses on producing quality, cutting-edge books for communities of developers, administrators, and newbies alike. For more information, please visit our website at www.packtpub.com.

About Packt Open Source

In 2010, Packt launched two new brands, Packt Open Source and Packt Enterprise, in order to continue its focus on specialization. This book is part of the Packt Open Source brand, home to books published on software built around open source licenses, and offering information to anybody from advanced developers to budding web designers. The Open Source brand also runs Packt's Open Source Royalty Scheme, by which Packt gives a royalty to each open source project about whose software a book is sold.

Writing for Packt

We welcome all inquiries from people who are interested in authoring. Book proposals should be sent to author@packtpub.com. If your book idea is still at an early stage and you would like to discuss it first before writing a formal book proposal, then please contact us; one of our commissioning editors will get in touch with you.

We're not just looking for published authors; if you have strong technical skills but no writing experience, our experienced editors can help you develop a writing career, or simply get some additional reward for your expertise.

Learning Ionic

ISBN: 978-1-78355-260-3   Paperback: 388 pages

Build real-time and hybrid mobile applications with Ionic

1. Create hybrid mobile applications by combining the capabilities of Ionic, Cordova, and AngularJS.

2. Reduce the time to market your application using Ionic, that helps in rapid application development.

3. Detailed code examples and explanations, helping you get up and running with Ionic quickly and easily.

Mastering Android Application Development

ISBN: 978-1-78588-422-1   Paperback: 298 pages

Take your Android knowledge to the next level with this advanced Android application guide, which shows you how to make even better Android apps that users will love

1. Learn how to design and build better Android apps to reach new users.

2. Explore the latest features and tools in the Android SDK that will help you become a better developer.

Please check **www.PacktPub.com** for information on our titles

PhoneGap 4 Mobile Application Development Cookbook

ISBN: 978-1-78328-794-9   Paperback: 356 pages

Build real-world, hybrid mobile applications using the robust PhoneGap development platform

1. Get to grips with the usage of PhoneGap and its command-line interface.

2. Learn to use numerous plugins to access several hardware capabilities.

3. Step-by-step instructions on creating captivating mobile applications using popular frameworks.

Android Studio Cookbook

ISBN: 978-1-78528-618-6   Paperback: 232 pages

Design, debug, and test your apps using Android Studio

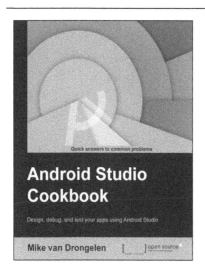

1. See what Material design is about and how to apply it your apps.

2. Explore the possibilities to develop apps that works on any type of device.

3. A step-by-step practical guide that will help you build improved applications, change their look, and debug them.

Please check **www.PacktPub.com** for information on our titles

www.ingramcontent.com/pod-product-compliance
Lightning Source LLC
Chambersburg PA
CBHW060137060326
40690CB00018B/3913